I Never Planned It That Way

Also By James O'Hara

IN THE LAND OF SHIVA, A MEMOIR

I Never Planned It That Way

Accidental Soul Work
On the Road and at Home

James O'Hara

Leandros Publishing

Leandros Publishing
www.leandrospublishing.com

ISBN 978-0-9912416-2-0 (Paperback)
ISBN 978-0-9912416-3-7 (Kindle Ebook)

Leandros Publishing
Berkeley, CA

Author Photo: Johanne LaRoque

Printed in the United States of America

For All My Teachers, Again

You are of all ages, ethnicities, races,
gender identifications, sexual orientations.

You comprise the rainbow that leads to the
great treasures of life, a veritable pot of gold.

Table of Contents

2011

Delhi, Nepal, Cambodia, Myanmar

2016
Vietnam and Laos

2021
USA

At the Train Station

Northern India
1980

THE FLIES WERE to blame. Had it not been for the oversized black flies I wouldn't have seen it. I cannot blame my peripheral vision which was just doing its job of noticing movement.

I had approached the outdoor ticket window at the edge of the train platform and asked for a first-class ticket to Patna, several hours to the west. While the agent dithered about, I caught activity out of the corner of my eye, to the left. A swarm of large flies circled something off the platform down on the ground so I leaned over to look.

A decapitated body lay there.

The head was there too, but nestled—along with the severed hands—in the bloodied folds of the man's *lungi*, a wraparound, between his knees. Blood matted his hair, and the eyes were open.

I must have taken an audible breath in, for the Indian man behind me cleared his throat and spoke to me in English.

"Yes, it is terrible to see. So sorry for you."

"But what happened? And why is the body just lying there?"

"I do not know what happened, but we must wait until nightfall when men of the proper caste will take it away."

I wanted to ask why the need to wait, why can't he at least be covered up, and a dozen other questions, but the agent held my ticket and was expecting payment. I gave the money, accepted whatever change he handed me, and went to sit on a bench.

Though the sight of the body had been shocking and I could not get the image out of my mind, surprisingly I wasn't nauseated or weak-kneed. More than the physical details of what I saw, what unsettled me most was the idea of a dead body lying there in the open, attended to only by those damn flies, while people casually purchased their train tickets or munched nearby on the sweets offered by the many platform vendors.

But this was India and an approach to death I was not familiar with.

Death was not shielded from public view in India. It wasn't uncommon to see four men shouldering a pallet containing a dead body walking down the street on their way to the cremation grounds. No special permit was needed here to transport the dead, no special attire required for the occasion. In their *lungis* and sandals, the bearers nevertheless had serious countenances.

At the cremation grounds—which I had visited but stayed at the periphery—the family stands near the funeral pyre and watches as flames engulf their loved one, eating away first at the clothes and then the person's flesh and bones. Hopefully the family could afford enough firewood for a thorough burning, for when the fire burned itself out, ashes and whatever else remained were cast into the river.

Who of us in the U.S. has watched the cremation of a loved one? Who has carried the jostling body of a friend on our shoulders? American pall bearers carry a closed casket which might contain a large log for all they know. We are quite separated from the stark realities of dead bodies.

I am not opposed to the average American way of treating death and funerals. But there are excesses recorded more than two generations ago by writers such as Evelyn Waugh and Jessica Mitford. Mitford specifically railed at how American funerals are too sentimental, highly commercial, and excessively expensive. Not much has changed since the publication of her book, *The American Way of Death*, in the 60s.

Surely our plethora of laws concerning disposal of the dead include much that is helpful in terms of safety and hygiene for the living, and this is to be honored. But our customs do protect us from facing much of the unpleasantness of death.

I confess that I don't really want to face death so directly, but India gives me no choice.

The Global Classroom

FOR WEEKS I was haunted by the image of the mutilated dead man in the train station. I tried to distance myself from it, to no avail. So I looked inwardly for what else there might be—besides the apparent disrespect for that body—that I had found so striking.

Eventually I came to this: seeing an unadorned dead body, sans cosmetics, with its soulless presentation—*which we all grasp immediately*—leads us to understand that our essence *is* soul. Without soul, the body we inhabit is like a suit hanging in the closet, physical matter that can be taken on or discarded, or dropped and left to disintegrate.

But what is soul? How does one define it? Oh, definitions, definitions, the hobgoblin of logical and linear (and constipated) minds. (Apologies to Emerson.) A somewhat descriptive approach may serve us better. Consider calling soul *that part of us not limited by time and place and intrinsically connected to every other being.* The latter part of that sentence is the more key description.

Every religion or philosophy that I have studied comes to the same conclusion: we are not separate from each other, in fact we are bound together like threads in a single fabric.

Our job is to wake up to that reality. And we do get that, often in times of crisis. When we rush out in front of that speeding car bearing down on someone frozen in place by fear, it's because at a deep level—perhaps not yet articulated—we know that that person is us, we are that person. The challenge is to have that insight conscious and ongoing. That is soul work.

Said another way, to engage in soul work is to engage in any practice, path, or activity that enables us to transcend our physical self and personal ego. That's a mouthful, I know.

I often strolled the perimeter of the burning *ghats* on the banks of the River Yamuna—India's second sacred river—just blocks from my house in Delhi. I did not venture close in, but rather observed the smoke curl upwards from a distance. Like incense wafting toward the heavens, ash from wood and corpse reminded me of another basic reality. I too will die. Not someone else. I myself will die. That won't sound like new information but I admit I am one of those who "knows" that we all will die but secretly believes he will be the exception.

Those words have in fact become a mantra of mine. *I too will die. Not someone else. I myself will die.*

India smacks me in the face with death more often than I would choose, but then, when has choice ever been a factor in such a situation. An elderly lady in my Delhi neighborhood whom I had greeted daily for months quietly slipped away one day, and her street cot was immediately occupied by someone else. Her grandson informed me of her death the next day and the cremation that had already taken place. It was all too, too abrupt for me, and I was saddened by her passing.

What a Teacher India has been for me—sometimes an eager and sometimes a reluctant student. I had never seen death up so close and raw in America. The smoky air of a burning *ghat* is worlds away from green cemeteries dotted with marble statuary and Corinthian columns.

All of life's major lessons can be learned in one's own home and neighborhood, and I like to think I have accomplished quite a bit on home territory. It is also true for me that travel in foreign cultures has been a major vehicle for me to see life—and death—with fresh eyes.

I have continued to visit countries in South Asia and Southeast Asia over the years. I carry with me a plain copy book, and am at the ready to record both ordinary and sometimes extraordinary events encountered on the journey.

These musings—originally written as emails to friends while traveling, and since elaborated upon—along with reflections on events closer to the home hearth, are what I offer you.

Opportunities for growth in awareness meet us at every turn if we but open our eyes, our ears, and especially our hearts.

2002

Nepal, India, Thailand

Traveling Light

Pokhara, Nepal
October, 2002

DEAR FRIENDS,

There are few places in the world where you can sit in a semi-tropical area—banana trees and thatched roof open-air restaurants in the background—and gaze directly into 25,000-foot snowy peaks.

I am in Pokhara, Nepal's "second" city, where I am happily ensconced for a week, and am scribbling away in my copy book. Later I shall find a cyber-café and get these jottings off to you, Gentle Readers, and perhaps bring a hint of another world to you.

It is October, the monsoons have finished, the humidity is gone, and blue skies as well as green rice paddies present a treat for the eyes.

Pokhara is Nepal's trekking capital, located a mere five and a half-hour bus ride—or short plane flight—northwest of Kathmandu, and the nearby spectacular Annapurna range is the main draw. Even if you are not a trekker, sipping tea along the shores of Phewa Lake gives an often much-needed respite from the clamor of Kathmandu, the country's capital. But all international flights arrive in Kathmandu so that was my first stop on this trip back to Nepal.

Sometimes "winging it" is a boon.

At the Kathmandu airport I passed up the long line of travelers who had planned well and obtained their visas ahead of time, and stepped into the tiny queue for those of us getting airport visas. In no time I had slipped through Immigration as easily as ghee running down an oil lamp, and stepped outside into the distinctive air of Kathmandu—crisp, but not always clean. Nevertheless, it felt like "coming home" to me.

* * *

I had lived in Kathmandu from 1982 until 1986. At the time I was a brother in a Catholic religious order, and a group of four of us had been sent to India in 1980 to establish a branch of our order there. We were making headway in India toward that goal but, due to visa difficulties, I moved our headquarters to Kathmandu, Nepal.

The Nepal/India border is an open border for citizens of those countries, so we continued our work in India by maintaining a base in Kathmandu for training of the young Indian brothers, while visiting India ourselves periodically on tourist visas.

Living next door to Hindus, across the street from Muslims, and down the road from Buddhists and Jains and Sikhs, had a profound effect on how I began to view religion. It seemed to me that the religion that was the "truth" to an individual rested mainly upon which particular family they had been born into. I soon found myself standing at the edge of my Catholic cocoon, and I eventually left the Church and the Brotherhood in the late 80s, a few years after my return to the States.

While Christianity and being a Catholic Brother had been mostly good for me—in spite of my bristling about "blind faith" being a virtue—the time had come to leave it behind. I found myself in a place "beyond religion," with no adherence to any set of theological "beliefs." And I am quite comfortable, indeed energized, by that stance.

What I never left behind was the enchantment that I found in my journeys through Asia and contact with its diverse people. And that experience, even amid some-times-trying circumstances, pulled me back multiple times, where my travels provided not only additional windows into other cultures but also unexpected opportunities for growth in awareness, that is, soul work.

* * *

"Mr. James! Is that you? Is that really you?" a voice called to me from behind the wall of a gated home, the house I had rented years earlier in Kathmandu.

In spite of the years—I was now sixty-one instead of forty-four—my former landlord and I recognized each other and he invited me in to visit and see the house. And, of course, have tea. He had redone much of the house interior, though of course not as tastefully as *I* had furnished it. (Ego lurks nearby on an hourly basis.)

After pleasant conversation and sweet, milky tea, he walked me back down the driveway. He proudly pointed out that he, a Hindu, had maintained the shrine of Mother Mary that the brothers had created years earlier in the front yard.

"Yes, this is the Virgin Mary," he said. "I am still knowing her name, you see, and I think I will be blessed." I assured him he would be blessed.

Seeing the statue brought back a stream of memories of joys and challenges of times gone by, though I must say, no regrets about anything—except for the times I had lacked in compassion. A friend in the U.S. had once asked if I regretted the almost thirty years I had spent as a brother now that I was no longer even a Christian. I responded that I had benefitted greatly from those years, I had "grown up" as a brother, became a professional in the field of education, and had built many lasting friendships. I also felt quite good about myself and I knew that that "self" was the sum total of *all* past experiences I'd had, so no, no regrets.

I now consider myself as more universal in my spiritual outlook than any one religion can encompass, though I still understand the power of symbol and ritual to impact our lives and evoke the sense that there is more here than meets the eye. Catholic images—embedded in deep neural pathways—form the basis of my religious mother tongue and will always be windows to the transcendent for me.

As I left through the gate of that familiar yard, I inclined my head to the statue and let the Hail Mary that addresses the Great Mother float through my mind.

Several days later.

After visiting other friends and shopping for gifts, I walked out onto the tarmac in Kathmandu to the small plane that would bring me here to Pokhara—and my heart skipped a beat.

We were asked to identify our luggage before takeoff, but nowhere on the cart near the plane's stairway could I spy my suitcase. Twenty frantic minutes and fruitless searches later we took off without my luggage. It appeared that my suitcase full of life's necessities which had navigated three international airports the previous week without event would not make this twenty-five-minute domestic flight.

On the short flight I meditated on "detachment," telling the universe that, yes, I really wanted to learn that virtue but just not now. I suspected that Buddha Air was somehow going to give me a spiritual smack in the head, when all I wanted was to see the mountains and visit with a good friend, Ram, a porter for me on the Annapurna trek some seventeen years earlier.

I descended the shaky door-cum-stairway of the eighteen-passenger plane ("One person going at a time only, please.") in Pokhara, walked across a grassy area and saw Ram standing there, a bouquet of fuchsia roses (plastic) in his hand and sporting a wide grin.

A stalwart man of thirty-six now and a Sub-Inspector on the police force, he had gained access to the airport security area "to be the first sight you see in Pokhara," he explained.

"Roses are a sign of love, isn't it?" he stated as he handed me the bouquet. That image is fondly kodaked in my mind and his affection for me over the years is etched in my heart.

Inside the airport, underling security officers scurried to salute Ram while he ushered me through corridors, past baggage agents, and up to the "in-charge" who tried to reassure me concerning my luggage.

"No problem, no problem, this happens all the time."

That was not reassuring. After several phone calls, he confessed that no one could find the bag.

"I am thinking," he said in a noncommittal tone of voice, "that your bag was sent to the Indian border."

Gifts, and Raju the Room Boy

THE HIMALAYAN VIEW Hotel is a new, three-story guest house of perhaps ten rooms.

I am the only one here.

Tourism and trekking are down in Nepal because of the Maoist threat in the hills. (I will say more about the Maoists/Communists later.) My room is on the rooftop verandah, with windows on three sides—almost exactly like my old room in my Kathmandu home. I have views towards the lake on one side, and the mountains—the Annapurna range—on the other two sides. Although it was midday the mountains were still shrouded in cloud cover.

Another call to the airport and, wonder of wonders, my baggage had arrived from its side trip to the Indian border. So, how did it get on the wrong flight if all bags must be identified alongside the plane just before boarding and take-off? Dear Gentle Readers, this is Nepal.

Ram reported for police duty and I strolled this lakeside town, noting the variety of trekker services it offered: Romeo's Restaurant, Funky Boss Trekking, Kimchi Karokye [*sic*], Enlightened Yak Restaurant, Puja Momo Place (read "Holy Pot Sticker House"), Hotel Nirvana, Sacred Angel Bookshop, Resonable [*sic*]

Money Changer, Park and Shop Super Market, and Racy Shade Hotel (I don't get it either).

A fresh lemon soda—club soda, sugar, and lemon—at a small ants-in-the-sugar-pot restaurant refreshed my brow that had needlessly worried about the luggage. I'd like to think that on the flight down I had already "let go" of my baggage, both physical and metaphorical, and had learned my lesson about detachment. So, there was no need for the bag to really be lost. But that's probably pushing it. Maybe it was the three Hail Marys that I sneakily said to St. Anthony Finder of Lost Objects which did the trick. Or does it matter? That's the Zen question for the day: "Does it matter?"

What matters to me these days is that I function more and more from "intention," all the while being mindful that "ego" can sneak in there and create self-centered intentions. The best intentions thus seem to be ones such as, "My intention is to see with the eyes and heart of compassion," or "I intend to see each person as another thread in the Great Fabric I myself am a part of." Such intention setting is key to soul work.

While preparing for this trip I came across a book about travel and pilgrimage which spoke to my soul on every page, Phil Cousineau's *The Art of Pilgrimage*. This book is a must read for anyone who senses that their upcoming trip has more at stake than just the pleasure of seeing the world's beautiful and interesting places.

"The object of pilgrimage is not rest and recreation." So begins the Forward. What *is* the object of pilgrimage? It seems that the goal is revealed *as we travel*. As one pilgrim put it, "The *path* is the goal." What we learn is likely not the specific objectives we happily articulate ahead of time, but rather what is presented to us along the way, often in unexpected moments or seemingly accidental events.

But we can prepare for the pilgrimage. We can set general intentions that serve as our mental and emotional lighthouse as we navigate the sometimes-troubled waters of travel in distant lands.

I had set my beacon for this trip with the help of a time-honored oracle, the Tarot deck.

A Tarot deck, you might know, is a collection of cards with pictures, symbols, and sometimes words on them that relate to various themes of our lives. I don't see the act of pulling a card as fortune telling. To me the cards are more like a Rorschach test, images that elicit from the deep psyche different responses from different people, and various responses from the same person on separate occasions.

After much pondering, I came up with three questions related to travel and pulled a card for each from the deck.

Where shall I go? The Tarot card was the Priestess. "Go to holy places."

How long shall I stay in each place? The card drawn was Eight of Worlds—Change. "Stay until you are changed by the place."

What should I be mindful of? Four of Worlds—Anger, Frustration. "Use frustration, 'suffering,' as a signal that you have inner work to do."

With these guidelines written on paper and inscribed in my unconscious, I had begun this trip.

For "holy places" I put the sacred Hindu cities of Haridwar and Rishikesh on my list, as well as Bodh Gaya, the place where the Buddha is said to have attained enlightenment. Although those cities would be a focus for me, I do realize that the deep lesson is to see the "holy" in any place I visit.

What "change" will happen for me and how I will use inconvenience to focus on inner work remains to be seen.

* * *

Here at lakeside in Pokhara I can look directly at one of the more well-known mountains in the Annapurna range, Machapuchare. Literally it means "fish tail" though that aspect of it cannot be seen from Pokhara. In 1985, I was living in Nepal and was able, with Ram, to see it from the proper angle. It resembled a large fish which had taken a dive into an earthen mound, with only its tail visible, pointing skyward.

* * *

Two-thirds of all trekkers to Nepal visit the Annapurna area because of its easy accessibility. Comfy though basic guest houses dot the main trails and the scenery includes high mountains and as well as low-lying villages. In the villages, locals invite you to stay in their homes—for a fee—should you want more regional culture than you would find at a guest house.

Jimmy Carter was there that fall, staying at the upper-end Fish Tail Lodge on the other side of Phewa Lake, access to which was by raft only, poled by a hard-working Nepali. Ram, a nineteen-year-old, had seen me on the main road looking at the various trekking services offered. Hoping to earn extra cash, he introduced himself and offered to be my porter. I felt comfortable with him and the price was right. We were set to go.

A typhoon which had been brewing in the Bay of Bengal chose that moment to sweep across India into Nepal, and deposit unheard-of quantities of rain in Pokhara as it hit the

Annapurna range. No one could leave to go trekking those first two days of torrential rain. Nor the second two. Nor the two after that. Jimmy Carter gave up and relocated for a trek closer to Mt. Everest which had not been so affected.

The treacherous snow dumped on the upper altitudes caught those already on the trail by surprise. Among others, a group of snowbound Italians was stranded in a most precarious area: the Thorung La Pass at over 17, 000 feet. If they could safely descend, they would shortly reach Jomsom, a tiny airport at 8,800 feet, with air service to Pokhara.

With my time running out, I began fretting that the days I had carved out for a trek would be spent staring at rain from my lodgings. If I could fly up to higher altitudes and walk back, at least I'd have a bit of a trek, but all commercial air service had been cancelled indefinitely. In chatting with an airline agent one day, I discovered that a rescue plane had been chartered to pick up the Italians, who were expected to make it to Jomsom. The precious seats on the flight up were in great demand but I managed to obtain tickets for Ram and myself.

The next day Ram stared intently out the plane window, his first flight, and smiled when he spied his own home from the air. We reached Jomsom in twenty minutes, and the skies had cleared.

Things were now on the upswing. We climbed up to 12,000 feet to visit the temple at Muktinath revered by both Hindus and Buddhists. Ram stripped down to his boxers and stepped under the spigots of holy water to get a blessing. I could see the goose bumps on his back and chest—12,000 feet, remember? It seemed rather Catholic—suffer in the name of religion and this is beneficial for you.

The six-day trek back to Pokhara allowed me the space to enjoy the grandeur of the mountains and to meditate on my habit of constant worrying about my plans not working out. If I had needed to remain in Pokhara, I would have utilized the time well. I would have learned more Nepali words from the locals, or practiced my Hindi with Indian tourists. I would have figured out *something*. I always do, I just don't always trust that I will. It was time to buy into my own creativity. And the Annapurna range would be there for a bit longer should I miss it this time.

I enjoyed the quiet presence of Ram on the way back, and we had kept in touch over the years.

* * *

Rams' home is quite simple—three rooms connected by an outside verandah. Ram had brought me there to meet his wife, Urmila, and two small daughters. All three were charming if a bit shy. I presented the girls, Neha, 10, and Rosie, 8, with Hello Kitty purses I had filled with scented felt pens, glittery stars, heart-shaped stickers, and fluorescent plastic paper clips. (Paper clips? I liked the colors.). They pranced around the room like princesses carrying handbags of spun gold. I gave Urmila scented candles for the house and foreign cologne for herself. She'll probably never use the cologne but will put it in the window for the neighbors to see.

For Ram I brought a polo shirt and American jeans. He was thrilled, having spent his money on new clothes for his wife and children—a "must" for the upcoming Hindu High Holidays—but had bought nothing for himself. His salary is $60 per month and even though that can't really be compared to $60 in the U.S., it is still a meager income here for a family of four.

After a tasty Nepali meal of spiced chicken, lentils, spinach, and rice, I returned to my hotel, content to be near friends, in sight of the Himalayas, and breathing fresh air.

* * *

Not sure what day it is for I have lost track of time. I have left behind in the U.S. such energy-draining activities as clock watching, calendar marking, and detailed planning. I am here in part to rest my weary brain from such activity, though I occasionally must check the date to ensure I don't miss my flights.

I have established my morning routine. I wake around 6 a.m.—no biggie, having gone to bed at 10 p.m.—reach languidly from under the covers to draw back the drapes and see the Himalayas from the window. There are about eight peaks immediately visible, all of them over 20,000 feet. I keep saying "peaks" but you must remember that the view is not one of distant mountain tops but startling close-up visions of half the mountain itself.

The whitest peaks are ones with gradual slopes, and those that are darker have steeper slopes to which the snow cannot easily cling. The best example of a steep slope is Mt. Everest on the other side of Kathmandu from here. The next time you see a picture of that wonder, note how black much of it is.

* * *

Mt. Everest. Wasn't it rather self-referent of those Brits to name that sacred mountain after one of their own, a former Surveyor General of India? A quick look at history might encourage us to take a softer view on the matter.

One of the most complex undertakings of the nineteenth century, the Great Trigonometrical Survey of India was a project some thought would take five years, but in fact took almost 70 years. Dragging 1000-pound theodolites—devices for measuring angles in both the horizontal and vertical planes—around India for decades enabled the surveyors to establish an amazingly accurate map of that country. The survey started in South India in 1802, and years later when it reached the northernmost area the team was dismayed to find that Nepal, home of purportedly the highest mountain in the world, was closed to them. Nepal had suspicions of British political aggression or colonial dominance. Imagine.

Discouraged but determined, the survey team set up camp in the malaria-infested lowlands, the *terai*, where three officers died from that mosquito-borne disease. The team nevertheless measured Peak XV from a distance of roughly 150 miles, and in 1856 announced its height to be within twenty-seven feet of its current assessment of 29,029 feet. (Everest, however, continues to grow higher due to the continued crashing together of the Indian and Eurasian tectonic plates. It may even lose altitude during sizeable earthquakes.)

But, what to name it? The Royal Geographic Society in fact had a stated policy of naming landmarks using the local name. The only information available to the British, however, was what various travelers from that region brought into India—and apparently there were numerous local names. Not wanting to name the mountain after what might be just one tribe's appellation for it, the Society settled on Everest in honor of George Everest, a former director of the survey. Everest himself opposed the idea, but it won out.

Today the name Sagarmatha is used widely in Nepal, but it is of very recent origin. No doubt an older name for that famous mountain is the Tibetan one, Chomolungma, which some say means "Holy Mother" but which supposedly one Tibetan crone said simply meant "fat hen."

The name Everest is likely here to stay.

* * *

Each morning here in Pokhara I crawl out of bed and call for Raju the Room Boy to bring me morning coffee. He is anxious to serve. I am his only duty and he would surely get bored if I didn't send him on errands. Today he has already wiped the morning dew from the table and chairs on "my" verandah, so I sit there, sip coffee, gaze at the mountains, and read a bit.

An hour or so later I go off to American-run Mike's Restaurant for the Cholesterol Special: a cheese omelet and fried potatoes with slabs of bacon floating in grease, and Berkeley-strong coffee. Mike's is not only right on the lake, but plays lyrical Nepali music instead of blasting American rock music the way the Nepali cafes do. Go figure.

Nightly dinner is with Ram and his family, after which Ram and I go out for a walk and a glass of wine.

Where does the day go? I don't know. I gaze, laze, and haze out in this wonderful place. I sleep a lot too. I am tired. America and work are behind me for now. Asia so far has been kind and not given me a boo-boo stomach—thanks be to Vishnu for bottled water—though I am still trying to get over a sore throat that started in California. So, I lie around Nepal, healing from something I brought with me from America.

This morning I was locked in.

I had walked across the verandah to call down for coffee, but the door to the stairs was bolted from the other side. I banged on it and a few moments later Raju the Room Boy unlatched it.

I asked him why he had done that and his eyes narrowed while scouring the neighborhood from our rooftop.

"*Chor*," he whispered. Thieves. Mind you, the bolt is on the outside of my floor and any thief could have slid it back as easily as Raju and stormed my parapet. There is no bolt on my side to keep thieves out.

Raju looked so pleased with himself I decided not to mention anything about it at the moment. The action baffled me. But why should I think that a measly seven years living in this part of the world should equip me to understand Asian ways?

All around my hotel birds chirp, caw, and coo. Dogs bark, babies cry, and roosters crow not only at dawn but when they know I am taking my afternoon nap. Small boys race down the street attempting to launch kites and nearly trip over the scrawny hens that scratch at the side of the road. Forget zoning laws, chickens have to live somewhere.

So, how do I sleep at night? I packed that item I recommend on the list of essentials for all travelers coming to any part of Asia: ear plugs. Walgreens had an economy pack of twenty-five pair. I won't need them all but if money runs low, I can auction off that spongy gold to desperate travelers.

Raju just came up to change the linens. I told him not to bolt me in tonight. *What if there was a fire?* A few minutes later he asked me, jaw quivering, if I was angry with him. I put my arm around his shoulder and assured him that I wasn't angry, and told him that the two bathroom towels he had arranged on the bed in diamond shapes looked quite lovely. He relaxed.

I already know half the town, thanks to Ram. He certainly knows everybody. He jokes with the men, makes *namaste* to the elderly, and kicks a soccer ball with little kids. If we want to go for a ride he flags down a passing motorbike and talks the owner into letting us borrow it for an hour. The bike owners agree not just because Ram is a policeman but because he is truly liked by everyone. He is on a voluntary security force for the neighborhood and donates his extra time to coach youth soccer teams. He is a genuine, good-hearted, native son.

Ram is not, however, without ambition.

He looks at me with soulful brown eyes, his hand over his heart and says, "Of all the foreigners I know I love you the best and can you get me a visa for America?"

He and many Nepali men would (temporarily) leave wife and children in a heartbeat for the land of riches and opportunity. He is convinced that if he came to America for two to three years, he would return to Nepal a wealthy man. There is an element of truth in it. A good number of Nepalis do indeed overstay their tourist visas in the U.S., work in restaurants, and send home money to their family. But there is more uncertainty. Might they be reported to the U.S. government before amassing a fortune? And can they really sock away the big bucks on a busboy's wages?

I don't exactly discourage his dreams, only tell him that I have no special power with the U.S. government—which is extremely hesitant to grant visas to people like Ram for the very reason that he wants it. I am more desirous of gathering U.S. funds to send his girls to a good school instead of the less-than-mediocre one they now attend. I told him and Urmila this, and their eyes brightened.

Nepal—like so many Asian countries—is a man's world. The woman is of consequence mainly through her husband, and only really so if she produces a son. If not, she may become an object of scorn and a mere servant in her husband's home. Or, Shiva forbid, in the house of her mother-in-law where her son might still live. The science of genetics which tells us that the male determines the gender of the embryo has no weight here. It's the woman's fault if she produces "only" girls.

To be fair when assessing this attitude, one must take into account that when a daughter grows up and marries, she becomes part of her husband's family and cannot assist her own family of origin. A son will take on that responsibility, an essential role in countries with no "social security" system. Both parents, then, fervently hope for a male child.

Other than a solid marriage, the main asset that a woman might possess to become more independent is to be highly educated. If I can give this family any lasting gift, I think it will be the education of the girls. While Ram was thrilled to hear my idea and truly appreciative, I could still see the lines of worry on his face—about another issue.

As a policeman, Ram has a dangerous job, not because of local thieves and bandits, but because of the Maoist insurgents.

In the mid-90s the Nepal Maoists—Communists—stated their goal, backed by rifles, of a "people's democracy" for their country. They saw their movement as a historical revolt against feudalism and the monarchy which they view as corrupt. Because the police are seen as tools of the government they have been targeted by the Maoists, and Ram has viewed the bloodied bodies of too many of his friends. Already twenty of the one hundred participants in his initial training class of sixteen years ago are now dead. Can you blame him for wanting to escape it all?

Last night at dinner, he appeared upset from news at the police station but wouldn't mention it in front of his girls. "Let's go for a glass of wine," he said.

Danger, a Massacre, and Festival Games

AT LAXMAN'S RESTAURANT, Ram sipped wine with me. Like most Nepalis he would prefer beer but it gives him a headache. "And I have a big enough headache already," he said. He had just received a fax from headquarters in Kathmandu warning him about letter bombs that the Maoists have started to use. Two police stations in the capital had already been targeted and hit.

"These are my friends being killed! And when I saw last month the widows of my companions dressed in white all I could think of was my wife like that and my children crying. What is all this for? What about my wife and my children? And myself?"

These are questions for which I had no answer, and it saddened me deeply.

Finally I urged him, "If you are assigned to a remote area where the Maoist threat is greatest, resign your job immediately. Somehow you will find other work or people I know will assist you in getting employment."

To my relief he replied that he had already discussed that possibility with his wife and they had both agreed he would quit the police force in such a case. He is only twenty-three months away from retirement—eighteen years is required—but even if he had just one month left and was assigned to a dangerous area, he would resign. It was encouraging to hear that he discusses important matters and decisions with his wife, which is not always the case with Nepali men.

Is this dilemma of care for one's family versus fighting for the country not an age-old issue for men? The problem is more clouded when you understand that, while the terrorist tactics of the Maoists are reprehensible, their struggles are born out of real injustices. For too many years both politicians and certain members of the royal family—though not the king himself—have creamed off foreign funds designated for the people. The rural areas have not received the education or health benefits that are now available next to the sprawling homes of the elite in Kathmandu Valley.

The owner of Laxman's joined us at our table, and the conversation not surprisingly veered toward the incomprehensible tragic events of the previous year—the massacre of the royal family at Narayanhiti Palace in Kathmandu on June 1, 2001.

"The prince would never kill his parents!" Ram cried. "Someone was there with a mask on that looked like the prince. Everyone says this."

"Ram," I said gently, "several family survivors have publicly stated that the gunman was the Crown Prince. Surely they would know him from a person with a mask."

"But he would never shoot his sister, Princess Shruti. He couldn't."

* * *

Few narratives could be as chilling as the various and often conflicting accounts of what happened that fateful Friday when the extended royal family had assembled for their monthly dinner.

According to one report Crown Prince Dipendra had been drinking heavily and was told by his father, King Birendra, to leave the gathering. Most other witnesses say that before the king arrived, the Crown Prince's brother, Nirajan, and two others had ushered him out of the room because he was acting half-drunk. The men had left Dipendra in his room, but he returned to the billiards room a short half hour later dressed in combat fatigues and carrying assault rifles.

The Crown Prince was a known gun aficionado, so no one was surprised at his costume and the weapons he carried. He had often roamed the palace grounds and shot at stray animals and birds.

As the king stepped forward to greet his son, the evening's host, the prince shot him at close range and then abruptly left the room. But he returned moments later with another gun and ammunition. The family was focused on the injured and dying king and was taken by surprise when Dipendra came back. His favorite uncle, Dhirendra, approached him, talking soothingly to him, but the prince fatally shot him in the stomach. Then Prince Dipendra fired from close range at several of the nearly two dozen family members present.

Going deliberately from one to the next, he killed his aunt Princess Shanti, his aunt Princess Sharada and her husband, his sister Princess Shruti, the king's cousin Princess Jayanti, and injured others. Several people hid behind a sofa, others huddled in fear during the fast-moving event, and one of his cousins survived by playing dead after being wounded.

When Prince Dipendra left the room for the last time and headed toward the garden, his mother Queen Aishwarya and younger brother Prince Nirajan went after him to confront him. First he shot Nirajan, who had attempted to shield his mother and who then received over twenty bullet shots, effectively leaving him a pulp of flesh and lead.

According to several witnesses the queen then shouted, "What are you doing? You have killed my whole family, now you must kill me!" He fired at her multiple times, shattering her face and skull so badly that at her cremation it was covered by a China doll mask.

The official account then says that Dipendra went to a small bridge over a pond in the garden and shot himself. All told, ten royal family members died as a result of that night's rampage.

Rumors had spread, many of them denying that the Crown Prince could have done such a deed. Other stories claimed there must be a conspiracy involved—either of local or international origin. These versions continue to spread.

What could have possibly motivated Prince Dipendra to engage in such carnage? In addition to information about his drug use, accounts eventually unfolded about a serious rift between him and his parents over his choice of a wife. For various reasons, the young woman in question was not considered a good candidate, especially by the queen.

Some said the queen objected because the young woman's family had close family ties to powerful people in India, and potential influence from India was not desirable. Others said the objection was the girl's being from a rival branch of the queen's own clan. Most royal family members, however, claimed there were "caste impurities" in the woman's background and that the queen was simply following protocol and tradition. The King apparently was also against the match, but was a more soft-spoken person. Were Crown Prince

Dipendra to marry someone of a sullied caste, he might have to relinquish his right to the throne, and that would have been unacceptable to Dipendra.

Reporters reminded the public that the Crown Prince had been disenchanted with his father since the mid-90s when the king had capitulated to demonstrators demanding a more democratic government and a constitutional monarchy. The Crown Prince apparently felt the king had given away "the family store," well, actually *his* store.

From early on, the Crown Prince had been told that he would one day be an absolute monarch like his father, even an incarnation of the god Vishnu. As a boy he had informed his teachers that they "couldn't tell him what to do" and had even slapped one of them. His upbringing had encouraged him to think he could have whatever he wanted.

One theory was that he only intended to kill his father, but drugs and adrenalin caused events to wheel out of control. With King Birendra dead, Dipendra would then be king and could do anything he wished, including marrying the woman of his choice. In the perverse logic and protocol of that royal family, as king he could not be charged with any crime. The royal family would be forced to rally around him and perhaps even make up a story about an "accidental" shooting.

Two ADCs to the royal family, members of the military whose job was to ensure their safety, later said they "just couldn't" have pulled a gun on the Crown Prince even if he had aimed a firearm at them. "We would die saluting him," they both said.

The current king is the younger brother of the murdered king. Gyanendra was the one senior royal not present during the massacre, giving rise of course to more conspiracy theories.

The truth of all this turmoil may never be totally known, but for many people in Nepal the events of a year ago have scarred their psyche deeply.

* * *

Saturday, not Sunday, is the weekly holiday in Nepal and because it is also the festival season, the day dawned with a playful mood on the faces of the locals, including Ram. Even the shopkeepers who cater to the trekkers heading out toward Annapurna opened their doors later in the morning and closed them earlier.

Ram and his friends organized games in the local park. I roamed the area—the only Westerner there—and watched Ram referee Tug of War and Shot Put. No one questioned Ram's decisions—he is both well-liked and respected by his peers.

Before the soccer tournament, the big event of the day—which would culminate in the winners receiving a plump goat for sacrifice—the coaches played an exhibition game. Ram was by far the best player. Do you think I'm prejudiced in his favor? Let me remind you that for several years I was a high school soccer coach and so have a trained eye in this matter.

I bought peanuts to shell, visited the Hindu temple nearby, and took pictures of the crowd and the prized goat. Many families will sacrifice a goat this week as part of religious rituals. The animal doesn't die in vain—it is taken home for food.

I read in the Kathmandu Post that people can order a sacrificial goat online these days. The website is quite popular with Nepali expatriates who want to gift their families back in Nepal with a festival goat for sacrifice. It's like wiring flowers.

My sore throat has finally faded away like pre-dawn clouds on Annapurna and my legs no longer feel as if I'm dragging bags of rice behind me. It has taken a while, but everything takes longer here.

Ram's extended family—in-laws, nephews, nieces—have all gathered at Ram's brother's home for *bara puja*, big sacrifice, and a goat waits tied to a stand of bamboo next to the house. My legs, which I thought were quite strong, now feel weak again.

Animal Sacrifice, and Tikka

THE TETHERED GOAT, its eyes staring blankly ahead as if it knew its coming fate, was in startling contrast to its energy earlier in the day.

That morning Ram, his brother, and I had gone to the bazaar to select the proper goat. Well, they selected while I photographed this particular brand of the merchandizing of religion. Goats bleated in bamboo pens, different colored markings made sure that one herder's animals didn't get mixed up with another's, and small children hovered nearby to sell a rope for the victim's neck.

Ram picked up several frisky goats to feel their weight and the meat on their bones. We then crammed the chosen animal and Ram's brother into the back of a taxi and sent them home. I needed Ram to accompany me to another section of the market where I purchased frames for my glasses which had spontaneously broken on the jostling bus ride to the bazaar. Instead of $200 frames, I now have $5 ones that look the same.

Back in the courtyard at Ram's brother's home, the local butcher was hired in order to have a clean kill. He wet down the hair on the goat's neck, raised his *kukri*—the curved Gorkha knife of war and worship—and severed the head in one swift slice. Ram, who had gripped the goat by the horns, collected its blood in a pan and helped dip the goat into scalding water to remove its hair. (Yes, ghouls, I have a picture of a blood-spattered Ram holding the severed head).

I sat down—certainly not weak-kneed, just tired—and was offered tea to sip and a place of honor from where I could best observe the butchering process. Hmm, enough detail for now. Well, one more thing. A half hour later Urmila served me delicious fried rice, and then asked if I wanted a special treat. She scooped brown-black curdles of something onto the rice as Ram explained that it was fried blood from the goat. Don't bother asking me what it tasted like because I did my best to block out all sensation and imagination for the next three minutes—and graciously declined a second helping.

On the tenth day of the festival of Dashain—the triumph of good over evil—families gather in the mornings for gifts of money and to receive a blessing from their elders in the ritual of *tikka*. *Tikka* is a mixture of rice, yogurt, and vermillion that is placed on the forehead by the one giving the blessing.

I arrived at Ram's in my shiny best, freshly pressed clothes, knowing that Ram's family would be decked out in their finest. (The previous day, I had sat in my T-shirt and shorts behind the counter of a tiny, dark shop, while a young Nepali man whistled a tune as he ironed my clothes—using an ancient instrument housing live coals—outside in the bright sunlight.)

Urmila wore a pink sari softer than puffs of clouds, the girls had on their best jeans (considered dressy here for youngsters) and Ram was decked out in freshly pressed dress pants, shirt, and tie. His mother wore a royal blue sari as befitted the clan's matriarch. The mother is in her seventies, though you might guess from her wizened face that she is in her late eighties.

Incense, flowers, food, shoots of corn plants, and a bronze stemmed platter holding the red paste adorned the living room table. Several Hindu figures grace the wall in Ram's home though by far the largest religious icon in the room—and their favorite one—is a glass-framed picture of St. Joseph holding the child Jesus.

Ram's mother first gave *tikka* to me, after which I presented her with an envelope of money. As the next oldest, I gave *tikka* to Ram, his wife, and children. They reciprocated and showered me with gifts of a T-shirt, a cap, a sweater, and a ritual brass water pot. I've seen these pots sold in the market by weight, using the ancient balances such as Justice holds in her hands. I was truly surprised by the lavish gifts and was happy I had given them well-packed envelopes of money.

Later in the day Ram and I went to the lake where he talked an acquaintance into loaning us a boat. We took turns rowing, enjoying the cool air and the lazy afternoon on the water.

Darkness had closed in almost completely as we passed the island temples in the middle of the lake and headed back toward the dock. It was probably the darkness that confused a boat passing by full of Indian tourists. They spoke to me, not Ram, and asked in Hindi if the temples were closed. I answered that they were. Later, another person asked Ram, "Who was that Brahmin you were with?" referring to me. Brahmins are high caste and of lighter complexion. Perhaps my skin tone, as well as dark hair and dark mustache, is why I have often been mistaken for a North Indian. I seem to morph into a local over here.

The following day brought the inevitable goodbyes to Ram's family, after which he and I left for the airport. Again he managed to enter the secure areas and see me off almost at the plane's door. He forced a smile, but it was far from the beaming welcome of a week earlier. I also felt sad upon leaving, but I know that all things fade away, both the joys and sorrows of life—the great Law of Impermanence.

Old Friends, New Friends, and Bodh Gaya

PATNA, NORTHERN INDIA

From time immemorial, travel has been fraught with discomfort, difficulty, and even danger. My first contact with India this trip was not dangerous, but depressing.

As the nighttime scenes in Patna slid past the taxi window, great disappointment settled on me concerning this country.

Was there no hope for a livable city in India? Patna: garbage heaps so large they crowd out one full traffic lane, dimly lit bazaar stalls with shrouded customers fingering goods and arguing with vendors, music blaring from special loudspeakers erected for festival time, and horns blasting from every bus and truck. To pass a vehicle, you must honk your horn so they will give you a few inches on the narrow street. And this scene is saturated with the smell of urine and cow dung mixed with sweet incense wafting from most shops.

And the lack of light. Patna, a state capital, has both regular and irregular power cuts and even when the current is flowing it is pathetically feeble. You can gaze directly at the bare bulbs that hang in the bazaar stalls and not hurt your eyes. The filament barely reaches a moderate shade of orange.

But all the above dims in comparison to the heart-rending sight of those raggedy youngsters with matted hair who stare longingly at a fruit stand, often with an even younger sibling squalling in their arms. It is again, oh so painful to see.

I had returned to an India of many fond memories but found only a discouraging scene. Had I blocked out this side of India's face? Partially.

When I look back on those India days in the 80s, what I recall most was the sense of creativity and adventure I experienced in accomplishing my goal of starting the Brotherhood there, and the heartfelt interactions I had with so many Indian friends as well as strangers along the path. The blistering hot days, the sicknesses, the maimed beggars at the train station, and all the evidences of great poverty strewn over the subcontinent—all this is remembered, but no longer with the power to completely upset me. I cannot have that or I would become depressed and emotionally paralyzed. Is my selective focus a Pollyanna attitude, a basic defense system, or healthy perspective? I suspect it is a bit of each but I would not do myself nor you a service, nor acknowledge the reality of the Indian subcontinent, to be in any way dismissive of its tragic side.

That astute observer, Ruth Prawer Jhabvala, a European married to an Indian—and a talented novelist, essayist, and the screenwriter of the Merchant Ivory team—compares residing in India to living on the back of a large lumbering animal: the heavy poverty of India which permeates every moment and corner of that land. She suggests that the only way for Europeans (in which category she includes Americans) to have a right to live there, is to be a doctor or social worker and make a contribution to India's people. This type of involvement brings reminders on a daily basis of the stark realities of the country and puts the very idea of comparing Indian and Western cultures out to pasture. There is not time for such mind prattle between bandaging wounds or supporting women's rights at the risk one's own life or limb.

Jhabvala's essay "Myself in India," the Introduction to *Out of India*, I believe is the most insightful and deliciously written post-Raj assessment in the English language of a Westerner living in India.

It begins with the classic lines: "I have lived most of my life in India. My husband is Indian, my children are Indian but I am not, and less so every day."

Patna has brought all those poverty-based realities back to me like a smack on the side of my head.

I was in Patna to meet up with my old friend, Brother Richard, a Canadian who has my former job—Superior of the brothers in India—because that town is the main gateway to what is likely the holiest shrine in Buddhism: Bodh Gaya, the place where the Buddha attained enlightenment under the Bodhi tree.

I had assumed we would travel by bus but Rich said, "Oh no, not a bus, that would kill my legs."

A more than six-foot, gracious, outgoing man, he suggested the car-for-hire method, which overall worked well. For the next several days we had both auto and driver at our disposal, for about $25 per day, gas included. Yes, it was a good deal, but don't picture paved freeways and a shiny new Toyota with a cleanly dressed chauffeur. Ratchet all travel conditions down about twenty-five notches and that will do.

Rich, ten years younger than me, is someone I have known for over twenty years and we made good traveling companions. His seventeen years in India coupled with my history there gave us plenty to talk about, and our training as brothers equipped us to sit quite comfortably next to each other silently for long periods of time.

"I've written ahead to my old friend, the D.I.G. in Gaya," Rich said. In his various roles as religious Superior in India, Rich had made numerous contacts with local officials and we were headed to visit one of them near Bodh Gaya. A D.I.G., Deputy Inspector General, is in charge of the police force for one or more entire districts in a state. In other words, a big shot.

Our car trundled down a broken road generously called a National Highway, past the Barabar Caves (the "Marabar" caves of Forster's *Passage to India*), and into the shabby town of Gaya, the district headquarters about five miles from Bodh Gaya. At a government office we picked up a police escort, necessary if we were to approach the home of the Deputy Inspector General.

Security was high at his residence and guards leveled rifles at our approaching car until the police escort shouted the secret password. It was *dost*, the Hindi word for friend, which didn't sound terribly secretive to me.

This particular Inspector, Nirmal, was in charge of the five most difficult districts in the state, areas plagued with banditry and gang wars, and as a former official in India's "FBI" he commanded not only power but great respect. Servants jumped to his every bidding, as did the officers under his command—while they executed a smart snap of their boot heels.

A tall, solidly built man in his late forties, Nirmal welcomed us and insisted that we have lunch with him. After a leisurely repast he announced, "I shall send a security force along for your visit to the shrine." Orders were barked, jeeps rolled out, extra officers summoned, more rifles hoisted, and a call made to the Chief of Police in Bodh Gaya to receive us properly. Nirmal also arranged for us to stay at the best hotel in Bodh Gaya, Japanese owned, at no expense to us. Who paid? I don't know. I suspect the hotel absorbed the cost, knowing that should they have an emergency the police would be quick to respond.

For the next three days every door, literally and figuratively, was opened for us. Meals were served, drinks poured, paths cleared as we approached any temple, beggars shooed away, and salutes rendered. What about the simple life that the Buddhist atmosphere would seem to encourage? I didn't care. I loved the convenience.

Back to the Buddha. Bodh Gaya is a small settlement in the midst of farmland and the area hasn't changed much for centuries. One could easily imagine ancient groups of Buddhist monks in their flowing orange robes making their way across the rice fields.

In the enclosed area of the Bodhi tree and temple, my skin prickled as I circumnavigated the shrine as per custom. That sensation was even more pronounced while walking under the Bodhi Tree itself, the police entourage about us notwithstanding.

Bodh Gaya's Chief of Police—a round-bellied man probably in his fifties—commented that Japanese visitors would unhesitatingly pay 5000 rupees (100 USD) for a leaf from the revered Tree. The branches were well above our head and the base of the tree was enclosed by an iron fence, so I knew that no visitors were hastily plucking a leaf for a souvenir. No leaves lay carelessly on the ground. Not being "without desire," I myself secretly wished for a leaf from the tree.

Bodh Gaya draws pilgrims to its environs, as opposed to tourists. Spiritual intent is evident on the faces of the hundreds of devotees, monks, and lay people alike who visit there. Some sit in meditation on the grounds, others walk one thousand times around the perimeter, and still others make countless prostrations to Lord Buddha. Though some activities may look like rote actions, I have no doubt that people are sincere. Being well away from the sightseers' route and a challenge to reach, the place has no groups of Westerners wearing shorts and snapping photos. In fact, I could count the Westerners I saw on maybe both hands, if I didn't include those in monks' or nuns' clothing. If you had no interest in Buddhism you probably wouldn't come here.

My interest in Buddhism stems from its simple premise. The Buddha—which means the Awakened One—was an ordinary human being, not a god incarnated or a divinely chosen prophet. Nevertheless, through meditation and reflection he found a way to rise above "suffering." That didn't mean that he was never inconvenienced or never in pain, but he just didn't "suffer" from it the way many of us do. It's a state of mind.

You might miss your bus and then wait serenely for the next one, or wait and "suffer" by getting upset, blaming others, drumming your fingernails—you might know this scenario. I do.

Say Yes to The Tea

Northern India, Early 1980s

The train came to a complete stop in the middle of a field just a few miles from my destination. A train in front of us had derailed but we would advance, the conductor said, when the track had been cleared—in about five hours.

But we were so close. Surely I could get there in less than five hours, though not by walking since the heat was stifling and I had luggage. While other passengers ordered tea from the vendors of a nearby village clamoring outside our coach, and pulled out decks of cards to pass the time, I grabbed my bags and left.

After a half hour of stressful and fruitless searching for taxis or buses in that remote village, I returned to the train. My travel companions were laughing and enjoying their card games, and one man offered to call the tea vendor back for me. I sheepishly sat down, focused on the amiable and peaceful scene in front of me, and said yes to the tea.

After the visit at dusk to the shrine we returned to the Inspector's home for late-evening dinner. The gathered party included the District Commissioner, a Hindu journalist, a Muslim business-man, his wife, and Nirmal and his wife. In true Indian fashion, the women left us men alone before dinner. We discussed every-thing from Buddha to Bush and had solved most of the world's problems by 9 p.m. in time for dinner.

Not surprisingly, Bush's Iraq stance came under fire, and being the sole U.S. representative I bore the brunt of serious—though never personal—challenges. I recalled the words of one of you just before I left the States, "You can always say you're Canadian," but the cat was already out of the bag. Large quan-tities of Scotch and brandy, however, soothed and smoothed international feathers that evening and by midnight Richard and I returned to our hotel quite content.

It was the next morning that I got my Bodhi Tree leaf.

Under the Bodhi Tree, and the Flower Sermon

OUR POLICE ESCORT to visit the shrine that morning had been downsized to one officer, a jeep, and a driver. I was actually pleased to not have an entourage with us during our more meditative time at the temple. We nevertheless appreciated the jeep and driver since our own driver had taken sick the previous night and had been whisked off to a doctor on Nirmal's directives.

After telling our attending officer to meet us at the shrine gate in an hour, Rich and I went our separate ways inside the enclosure.

Morning stillness pervaded the compound since only serious meditators had arrived at that early hour to sit under the Bodhi Tree. A few birds chirped in the surrounding trees, a monk chanted in the distance, and temple bells chimed periodically. My arms and legs again tingled and I felt rushes of energy surge through my body. I knew I was indeed in a "holy place."

Under the sprawling branches of the Tree, I sat myself down on the white marble covering the area. I had already scanned the area and no coveted leaves lay scattered about. Sitting cross-legged, I closed my eyes, breathed slowly, and enjoyed the peace of the moment. I did my best to practice the traditional meditation approach of simply observing my breath coming and going. And coming and going. Time passed.

I heard a soft noise. I opened my eyes and looked in the direction of the sound. There, a foot away, a newly fallen leaf lay on the marble. In slow motion I reached over, gingerly picked it up and placed it in my shoulder bag, not daring to wonder how this had happened.

The spade-shaped leaf is now carefully pressed in my travel bible, Lonely Planet's guide to India. I've been thinking of various ways to preserve that treasure, but came to the conclusion to simply let it deteriorate in its own time, another reminder of the Law of Impermanence.

Rich and I dismissed our attending police officer for our afternoon trip to Sujata's Temple, an isolated shrine in the middle of rice fields—though that proved to be a mistake.

Buddhist background, 6th century B.C.E. Sujata is the woman you see in Buddhist paintings who is offering a bowl of rice to an emaciated man, the soon-to-be Buddha. As a man of his times, Siddhartha Gautama had first sought peace/release/salvation according to the prevailing method of the day—renunciation. Many *sadhus*, holy men, wandered the land then as they do now, engaging in rigorous self-mortification that included near starvation, minimal sleep, eating garbage, and self-mutilation.

For six years the Buddha had lived in a cave not far from the Bodhi Tree, depriving himself and doing penance, but concluded that such renunciation had gained him nothing but a prominent ribcage and no sense of release from the prison of his desires. In accepting the rice from Sujata, a high-ranking woman of a nearby village, the Buddha gave up self-denial and proclaimed the Middle Way: no severe penances (yea), but no over-indulgence either (boo).

Shortly thereafter, on the night of the full moon in the lunar month occurring around March–April, while sitting under the Bodhi Tree the Buddha attained Enlightenment. I won't go any further into what that means right now. As if I could.

Back at 21st century Bodh Gaya, a friendly local guide, Bubloo, steered us across rice paddies and over small hills to the bucolic setting of Sujata's Temple. Serenity pervaded the air, only to be soon destroyed by the most aggravating, pestering, beggar children I have ever encountered—almost as promised by that third Tarot card I had pulled—anger, frustration. I hadn't fully appreciated how the presence of the police had prevented all such importuning earlier in the areas around the Bodhi Tree shrine.

My first reaction is always not to indulge beggars, since giving money to them merely brings on the other twenty scroungers hidden behind the rocks who have spotted a "soft touch." But if you don't offer them any rupees, the children whine and tap your arm the whole while you are in the area. After all my time in Asia I still don't know how to deal with beggars.

Bubloo did his best to placate the children and give them a rupee each from Rich and me, but still they lingered.

So, here's the question: was my irritation solely my own issue? Did the children have nothing to do with it? Would the Buddha have remained unruffled by those scalawags?

I swear to Shiva, as I wrote that last sentence on the outdoor bench where I sit, a mendicant came up asking for cigarettes—I have none—then asked for money. I gave him two rupees and he left. No strain. Now I wish I had given more to the children at Sujata's Temple. They were truly poor.

And, I must learn to choose generosity, at least generosity of spirit, to those who pester me. How to do that? I am not sure, but I suspect it is a habit of mind more than an individual decision made on each occasion. I shall keep the images of both the beggar children and that last mendicant in my mind, and let it do its work. Perhaps then I won't completely have missed the chance with the "accidental" appearance of the aggravating kids to do useful soul work. That "Anger" Tarot card had said, "Use frustration, 'suffering,' as a signal that you have inner work to do."

With our driver finally in better health, we took leave of Bodh Gaya and Nirmal—whom I presented with a book on Buddhism I was reading that he had admired—and headed home on a "loop" route in order to pass through two more important sites in Buddhism.

Rajgir is the site of the Buddha's famous Flower Sermon, given on a rocky hillside known as Vulture's Peak. The Sermon is a core one in Buddhist thought and it is said that the Buddha still delivers its message to all who will listen intently at that location. I wanted to find that spot.

Nirmal had called ahead to have a police escort waiting in Rajgir, which in fact again served us well. That particular day was the beginning of a special three-day festival and the city was thronged with Indian tourists. The attraction, besides the festival, was the immense Peace Pagoda that the Japanese had built on a high peak complete with the real thrill: a chair lift.

People arrived at the base of the lift in brightly colored *tongas*, those horse-drawn carts preferred by visitors. Our car zipped through all barricades with a salute. The police shepherded us past the long queue and we boarded the lift moments later. I felt guilty about our special treatment—for about ten seconds.

The Pagoda was impressive, but I mainly wanted to visit the place of the famous Flower Sermon. I asked several guards and guides where it was but no one seemed to know, and I had no idea what it was called in Hindi, nor did Rich.

Finally, I resorted to a proven useful tactic: ask one of the scrappy ten-year-old boys who sell postcards to tourists and whose survival depends on picking up foreigners' names for local places. Within minutes, we were on the proper trail to *Ghreed Kote.* It lay on a slightly lower peak marked by signs in Hindi and English as to the important site it was. But it was completely deserted.

While Indian tourists squealed on the chair lift above us and oohed and aahed farther away at the Japanese Pagoda, Rich and I meditated on the spot comparable to the hill of the Sermon on the Mount in Christianity. I was grateful the area was quiet, but it occurred to me that few Indians apparently were interested in an important piece of their country's spiritual heritage. True, Indians had mainly a Hindu background and Buddhism had long ago packed up most of its bags and migrated from its place of origin to countries like Thailand, Burma, and Japan. Thinking that everyone would naturally be interested in "sacred sites" was no doubt a naïve projection of mine.

I have known for some time that I am no longer a tourist, but a pilgrim. Touring has certainly been important, enjoyable, and useful to me in the past ("travel is broadening" is so cliché but so *true*), and I do not denigrate tourism in the least, I encourage it.

However, I myself am "toured out." Seeing interesting sights in themselves holds little attraction for me these days. Twenty years ago, I would have rushed to the pyramids had it fit into my schedule. Now, there must be an inner pull for me to venture afar, as is true of this trip to Asia. The theme of pilgrimage and taking time for personal reflection enlivens me on this journey, and I am ready for that.

* * *

The Flower Sermon

The Buddha appeared one day at Vulture's Peak where a large gathering expected him to give, as usual, a long discourse. Instead, he said nothing and simply held up a flower. Several disciples attempted theories as to what the flower symbolized but the Buddha still said nothing. As he walked among the crowd he came upon one disciple who also said nothing, and who just smiled and then began to laugh.

The Buddha said to the group, "What can be said I have already told all of you. What cannot be said I have passed on to this disciple." The disciple, Mahakashyapa, at that moment became the accepted successor to the Buddha.

The deepest truths cannot be put into words.

* * *

The ruins of the Buddhist University at Nalanda, another two hours from Rajgir, seemed at first a disappointment. Not offering much to see except a few brick walls and earthen mounds, it nevertheless became one of the most impressive experiences of the trip.

I tried hard to comprehend what the local guide said I was seeing as I walked about the area: a university that had lasted over 1500 years and had housed as many as 10,000 students at a given time now lay before me in ruins. Enough remains of the vast center to show outlines of classrooms, dormitories, kitchens, and dining areas.

How could it all have disappeared? This was a university, not an earthly kingdom to be conquered and destroyed. Even the guidebook suggests that you spend a half day walking the paths of the ancient corridors and meditating on the impermanence of all things.

Eventually Rich and I left behind us the silent echoes of thousands of footsteps at Nalanda and headed back to those things many of us stubbornly treat—in spite of all evidence to the contrary—as if they were enduring: our homes, our lives, our relationships, our beliefs.

Mother Gunga

INDIA IS NOTHING like my emails.

I paraphrase the opening words of Anne Cushman's book, *From Here to Nirvana—A Guide to Spiritual India.*

If it were, I should be feeding you false information and train schedules one year old, heat and dust and noise should pop out of your email, and you should be able to encounter sages and swindlers on the same yoga mat. My stories should evoke in you intense irritation and frustration but you should find yourself inexplicably enchanted and barely able to wait for the next email.

Here it is.

Haridwar and Rishikesh

Eons ago an Indian king petitioned the goddess Gunga to descend from the heavens and share her waters with humanity. Impressed by his many prayers and severe penances, she agreed. The force of her descent, however, would have destroyed the land had Lord Shiva not saved the day. He let her waters fall on his head and disperse through his matted hair, easing their way to earth and creating the five sacred rivers of India, of which the Gunga is primary.

The place where the Gunga/Ganges tumbles out of the Himalayas and onto the plains is considered to be Haridwar, one of Hinduism's most holy cities.

A four-hour train ride northeast from Delhi brought me, traveling alone now, to Haridwar around seven o'clock one evening. I don't like to arrive at a new place at night and with no hotel reservation but I had little choice. Short, stupid story: I had missed the earlier train by boarding the wrong one. The Delhi station had two trains with almost the same name on the *exact* same platform, sitting back-to-back since they depart in opposite directions. It looked like just one train to me. Luckily a fellow passenger explained the situation to me just moments before that train left the station. Frustration.

Wait, I guess I am supposed to settle into this annoyance and learn something, perhaps a lesson as basic—and repeated—as understanding that I don't have as much control over events as I'd like to think. (And that I need to engage in my actions with greater awareness.)

However, like the leaf falling from the Bodhi Tree, a gift was granted me because of the timing. When you go to Haridwar you *must* arrive at dusk as I did on the later train and take a cycle rickshaw from the station to the Teerth Hotel. What that means is that you travel in the open air through one of India's most colorful bazaars and see the Ganges in the shimmering light of a dozen temples lining its banks.

In the bazaar, bright lights illuminated mounds of pomegranates, papayas, bananas, apples, and shiny clusters of sweet dates. White sugar-and-milk squares filled large pans, woks of hot milk simmered on small burners, and little boys dropped batter into frying pans to make puff ball donuts.

And bangles, bangles, bangles. Shining circles of colored glass in every hue: crimson, emerald, turquoise, bright white, as well as silver and gold. To glance at the adjacent bangle stall was like turning a kaleidoscope a few degrees and getting shining new patterns to enchant the eye.

"Hello, hello," a young man called out and rushed over to my rickshaw. "Shake hands. Welcome India," he smiled. I thanked him and shook his hand before the rickshaw lurched to avoid a cow and continued on.

Around the next corner we entered the Street of Saris. Shopkeepers spread out one stunning garment after the other on a mat to dazzle their customers, as you've seen carpet sellers unroll their wares. The women shoppers tried to frown and not look impressed with the saris so they could bring down the price for "that average one"—which they coveted.

I say "garment" for sari, but a sari is in fact about seven yards of straight cloth with a width of perhaps three feet. The woman wears a halter of the same shade, multiple slips, and then wraps the sari about herself in a way that makes it look like a single flowing gown.

Just before turning the last corner, the sound of rushing water and chanting filled the air and then, there it was, the Ganges. Along its banks evening devotees dipped into the cold water, threw marigolds into the current, and chanted hymns, not surprisingly, to Shiva. The water rushed around rocks and platforms, eddied in pools, and lapped the shore—a wonderfully alive river.

I had seen the Ganges before, but only in the plains far to the east where its turgid waters bore debris of every kind, including human remains that costly firewood had not fully cremated and toward which mangy pariah dogs swam in search of a morsel for lunch.

Here, the Ganges was refreshingly clear. One Indian had told me that at Haridwar the river was so clean and holy I could drink the water. Don't worry, not for one minute would I try that.

A group of women leaned over the water's edge to set afloat cupped leaves that bore small candles. They became tiny boats riding the current and spreading sprinkles of light across the river.

At the Teerth Hotel, every room faced directly onto the *ghats*, the river banks, so on the following morning I could see early worshippers doing their ablutions. The river descends quickly at Haridwar so chains are strung out along the cement steps for people to grasp and not get swept away.

The hotel's name, Teerth, is perfect. A "*teertha*" is a sacred site, literally a "crossing" or "ford." Though no bridge spans the Ganges right there, visitors to this town know that with a dip into the Holy River you can cross over from the painful cycle of birth and rebirth to the opposite shore of liberation. I doubt if plunging my index finger into the chilly water the next morning did the trick, but I decided not to immerse myself fully and cross over to pneumonia.

Farther upriver another fifteen miles lies Rishikesh, yoga and guru capital of the world and my main destination. Many Westerners got their first glimpse of this hill town when TV cameras followed the Beatles there in the 60s as they found their guru and pursued Transcendental Meditation.

In Rishikesh, temples and ashrams line the river, and hills tuck this town in on all sides, making it one of the most pleasant places in India. The ashrams are often immense compounds, some park-like, which have a resident guru and a schedule of classes, talks, yoga sessions, chanting, and worship times. I chose to stay at the Green Hotel and not bind myself to a fixed routine.

The whole town here is strictly vegetarian—not even eggs are available. Guess what food is popular with Westerners? Italian. Pasta-based meals are offered everywhere here. I don't do well with wheat but happily I like vegetarian Indian food. Many Westerners, however, are baffled by the menus since they use only Hindi terms though written in English letters. How would a newcomer know that *mutter paneer* is "cheese cubes and peas in a tomato sauce"? My favorite is a South Indian dish available way up here in the North: *uttapam*, a thick sourdough rice/lentil pancake laced with tomatoes, onions, and chilies, and served with lentil soup and coconut sauce.

Yesterday I stepped into a restaurant where there was only one other customer, a Western woman, who looked decidedly ill at ease. She was engaged in a halting conversation with waiters who spoke almost no English. After overhearing her frustrated attempts to order food, I introduced myself and suggested she try *mutter paneer* and steamed rice. I then gave her a tour of the menu—from Brazil, she managed basic English as all foreigners traveling alone in India must—and wrote down key words on her notepad. She practically cried she was so grateful. She had subsisted on greasy fried rice, the only thing she knew how to order, for the last three days while taking classes at the Divine Life Society's ashram.

She told me that my kindness had just lopped off one nasty life for me from the turning of the Great Wheel of life, death, rebirth, life, death... Knowing that I had certainly not attained enlightenment (yet), I was pleased to receive that indulgence. I ran into her today and she in turn, went out of her way to show me a peaceful place to meditate along the busy river. A life off the Wheel for her, I hope.

Holy River, Holy Men, Holy Cow

YES, COWS DO roam the streets, block traffic, and yield products from their posteriors to be used as fertilizer and fuel. All over India, people seize upon this material, shape it into nice patties and plaster it on their outside walls to dry. The more feces you have on your house, the better off you are.

There remains, however, that period between bovine gift giving and the trip to the drying wall that proves a bit treacherous for us pedestrians. I thought I had mastered the art of hop-scotching through Rishikesh's narrow streets dotted with this raw material, but alas, I am imperfect in that skill. After an unfortunate foot placement one night, I observed irritation arising in me (note the Buddhist outlook in this Hindu town). Damnation! (Oh, I think that's the Christian ethos.) I could hardly truck through the hotel lobby like that but what to do? There were no grassy areas to serve as scrubbing mats and no water faucets nearby.

But there was one big source of water at hand—the River. Under cover of darkness I crept down to its edge but hesitated to ease my shoe in. The river was holy—would my action be desecration? Is disrespect only in the mind? If so, I was home free for I meant no affront. But the shoe was made of leather. Holy Dead

Cow! What if I were caught? Seriously, five Untouchables were lynched recently because they had slaughtered and butchered a cow—sold to them by Hindus.

Something had to clean my footwear and it might as well be the Ganges. Besides, it was only one shoe.

After the cleansing I snuck back to the roadway and headed toward the hotel. But as I eyed glistening peanut brittle at a bazaar stall, retribution struck and my other shoe found its way into holy mess. This time I shook most of it off and did the thorough cleaning in the hotel bathroom, for I dared not perturb Mother Gunga again.

* * *

I found my spot. Just five minutes away from my hotel and bazaar busyness, shade trees hang over cement benches that line the river's edge. It is there that I daily read, write, stare blankly into space, and breathe fresh mountain air. For variety and exercise, I wander the pathways along the river, visit the next town, and return.

A *sadhu* lives just behind my bench under a large tree and periodically we have a brief conversation in English. For someone who meditates quietly most of the day, his English is perfect, almost American-sounding, and makes me wonder what his educational background is.

A word about *sadhus*, the men who seek the Divine directly on their own and hope that their hard life will gain them great merit. They're everywhere in this area. In orange robes they walk the forest paths, line the streets of the town, squat in front of temples, and a few of them offer chillum for sale. Chillum here means a combination of tobacco and hashish although the word technically refers to the pipe itself. Signs in English and Hindi warn visitors to avoid such *sadhu*s, adding that a number of people have been murdered or gone missing after associating with them. I am not tempted to try chillum.

There are surely more *sadhu*s here per lotus pad than any place in India. I have a sneaking suspicion that foreigners and Indian devotees who come to Rishikesh are more generous in almsgiving than elsewhere. Generally, pilgrims are on a spiritual quest and giving to the poor is a time-honored practice for acquiring good karma. Somewhere I read that it is especially beneficial to give to the beggar who irritates you the most. I think certain beggars have read the same literature.

Actually I take that back, about Rishikesh anyway. Most *sadhu*s here don't actively beg but sit quietly with their palms open waiting for food or coins. Every day at noon, 20–30 of them line up near one particular temple for a free lunch of rice and lentils. There is another way to obtain food. Traditionally an educated *sadhu* will be an itinerant preacher who teaches the wisdom of the ages in return for his meals, though not for shelter. They sleep outside, sometimes on *my* bench.

A few embrace a life of severe self-denial, which the Buddha rejected, and one can only be amazed at the vast number of young men who go this route which includes celibacy. You might think the population of India is dwindling, but that is hardly the case. Almost no women are among these mendicants for such hardship is traditionally not seen as proper for females— although women labor in the fields, over the hot stove, and in soul-numbing factories.

"Hey, American guy. Come here, please," the *sadhu* behind my bench called to me. He asked if I would sit under his tree and ward off cows that might disturb his belongings while he went to the river for water. My first thought was, *but I could lose my bench spot.* Pettiness hovers ever so close. I obliged him after my initial hesitation.

I received my share of stares from both Indians and Westerners alike as I sat on the *sadhu*'s blanket under his special tree. I tried to look serene and enlightened—a Westerner who had "made it"—but mainly I shooed cows away.

The *sadhu* returned with an Evian bottle full of Ganges water, and I asked him about his chosen spot. He had been living under that particular tree for twenty years and at an earlier location for seventeen, with only his bedroll and a few clothes. Each morning he would get up, bathe in the lime-green river, do his toilet, exercise (he didn't say what that meant), and return to his tree to seek God (he didn't say what that meant either).

Why did he leave his other tree of seventeen years?

"Too many money-hungry *sadhu*s around that place. I don't like that. I trust only in God."

As I stood to return to my bench he said, "I could use thirty rupees for sandals." He was barefoot so I gave him fifty rupees and told myself that whether it was for sandals or not was none of my business. Once a gift is truly given, we have no say over it.

* * *

Is there something in Hinduism that appeals to me, just as there is in Buddhism? In one way, what interests me is the same in both traditions—the question of who we are and what "the divine" is. In the Advaita Vedantic tradition of Hinduism the individual soul is seen as a piece of cosmic Consciousness or God, Brahma, etc. We already are a *part* of god, not *like* god, and together we all constitute the Great Divine.

I have read about and pondered much on this concept, for it has been quite a startling notion for me given my early indoctrination in Catholicism. In that tradition it would be near blasphemy to consider oneself a part of God. No, we are *like* God and grow additionally so as "he" grants us more and more grace, especially when we attend Mass and receive Holy Communion. The all-good Christian godhead exists *apart* from us sinners and we can only pray, have faith, and do good works hoping to move in a bit closer.

To help me grasp the Hindu concept of the Divine mentioned above, I have been playing with this analogy of the human body and the Divine. All our body's cells, some scientists posit, display a form of consciousness. If we think of ourselves as those cells, you might be a white blood cell and I a red one, both of us aware vaguely of each other and the stream we flow in. But we have absolutely no idea of the greater being, the "person," that we are a part of, nor could we *possibly* imagine it given the limitations of our tiny cell-consciousness.

So too, each of us humans moves through life longing to know the greater reality out there—which our minds cannot grasp—and in our thirst for such knowledge we desperately do what we can: we make up definitions about what/who God is, what attributes God has, what "he" thinks and how he wants us to act. We even carry on about such things as the roles of "person" and "nature" in understanding what is called the Trinity (don't ask). But such invented "theology" is a sorry consolation prize for the real Divine.

Better to accept that we cannot describe the ultimate realities with words. I am reminded of folks coming off a "mystical" experience of LSD or the like, glowing like light bulbs, but frustrated because they cannot describe the experience. Of course not.

Whatever can be *said* about the great mysteries just isn't *it*.

* * *

"Do you mind if I sit here?"

An Australian girl, probably in her early twenties and traveling alone, sat down on a rock next to me. She ostensibly wanted directions to the post office but didn't seem concerned about getting there though it was almost closing time. After a few minutes of desultory conversation comfortably interspersed with silence, I guessed something. She simply wanted to be around someone who wanted nothing from her, and someone she sensed she could talk to easily.

"There's so much to see and do in India," she eventually said. "I'm afraid I'll miss something."

"You will, and that's okay. You'll get what you get this time and it'll be just right for you."

Later. "I think I'm being rude when I ignore the vendors and men on the street who keep calling to me."

"You're not. Everybody wants you. If you've said 'no thanks' politely, it is they who are rude when they pester you."

"Some men truly leer at me and I don't know what I'm doing to invite that."

"You're not doing anything. Because of films they think that all Western women, especially those traveling alone, are 'easy.' Try to remember, it's not about you."

A few minutes later, she rose and said, "Thanks for your time. I'll go to the post office tomorrow." She headed off to the ashram where she was staying, slightly lighter in her step I like to think.

Part of soul work for elders is to encourage youth along their path—whether they come to us by appointment or simply appear along the way—and perhaps impart to them a bit of wisdom. And we must not shy away from acknowledging that we have acquired insight, for that is available to all of us if we but reflect upon our experiences.

The psychologist James Hillman once said something like, "If today you (elders) have not encouraged at least one young person, you have missed your calling as an adult."

On my last day I collected all my loose coins and dropped them one by one into the hands of the *sadhus* lining my street. Next, I headed for a peaceful sandy beach along the Ganges. There I mustered up my resolve, stepped into the icy waters, and finally took the ceremonial plunge. In Rishikesh, one must do that.

Café Coffee Day, the Brothers, and the Ragpickers

THERE IS AT least one livable large city in India—Bangalore in the South. Known variously as "The Garden City," "City of Bungalows," "Little Rome" (due to the significant number of Catholic institutions), and "India's Silicon Valley," this burgeoning metropolis situated at 3000 feet is a site for sore lungs.

Though pollution exists it is moderate in this city's temperate climate, and the town's place in the country's growing tech industry guarantees that it has its share of Western amenities. Along Mahatma Gandhi Road, snappily dressed twenty-and-thirty-somethings sip cappuccinos and chat on their cell phones, 24-hour ATM's sprout everywhere, and Pizza Hut commands several locations. Levi's and Lee's compete on opposite corners, and theaters showing American films dot the town. In the streets, auto rickshaw drivers wear uniforms and actually use their meters (as opposed to gouging and bargaining), traffic signals work and drivers observe them. The lattes at Café Coffee Day are excellent and the chocolate mousse is orgasmic.

I have to ask myself if I am really in India. Yes, indeed. The muezzin at the local mosque gives a 5 a.m. call to the faithful, the smell of pungent incense wafts from small shops, skewed bamboo scaffolding fronts tall construction sites, and the aroma of coriander and cardamom fills the air at food malls. And unfortunately, Bangalore does not escape that all-pervasive and defining reality of India: abject poverty. Just drift away from the city center a bit and come upon, for example, the slums where the city's "ragpicker" children recycle urban trash.

As affluence in one sector of the population grows, so does their refuse in terms of recyclable materials. Ragpickers are those people, mainly youngsters, who scrape out a living by lugging their gunnysack full of waste from neighborhood streets to large centers for sorting, and gain a pittance from those agencies for their efforts.

Most ragpickers live in the slums. Their dark hovels line open sewage canals above which vultures wheel in search of carrion. The ragpicker children have little knowledge of how to care for themselves and hold scant optimism for their future.

There is, however, one small ray of hope. The community of religious brothers that I helped establish here in the 80s has grown, and one of their houses is right here in Bangalore.

Amidst the mounds of used plastic, aluminum cans, and squashed cardboard, the brothers teach the ragpickers basic hygiene, fundamental literacy, and how to manage a bank account in their own name. Without guidance, most would squander their earnings by the next morning on gambling and alcohol. Yes, that includes the ten-year-olds.

About sixty youngsters a year are offered the chance to be trained at the brothers' compound in carpentry, welding, or tailoring. Those who successfully complete the tailoring course are given a small sewing machine at graduation, and thus, the opportunity to move to the position of skilled worker and escape the slums.

"Jim, the seed you planted years ago has flourished and you should be proud," said Brother Victor, an Indian who joined the brothers during my time in India and who directs one of the Ragpicker Programs. The seed has indeed become a tree—and I am exceedingly proud. And simultaneously, humbled.

Why would one feel "humbled" when hearing how their efforts have borne fruit? I suspect it has to do with realizing that none of us creates a grand project all by ourselves. We are part of the larger network of efforts required to achieve the result. Yes, I know I gave special impetus to the project. I did my part, which was in large measure that of a "pioneer." That function requires a person who is not only capable of forging a path through an uncharted domain, but one who also gets energy from both the challenges and freedom that such a job is imbued with. I loved my pioneer role.

But I hadn't stayed with the mission for 15–20 or more years. That day-in-day-out task was not my cup of *chai*. Others have filled that role, others who might have buckled under the weight of a pioneer's tasks. I appreciate them and their contributions.

When we understand this dynamic of connection between all of us and the various roles each of us plays, we have entered the realm of the spiritual. All religions I have studied hold that at the deepest level, we are all connected. When one student asked the guru, "How then shall we treat others?" the master replied, "There are no others."

Besides the Ragpicker Programs, the brothers teach in rural schools, run clerical skills training centers, and administer emergency relief programs. Then, there are the brothers themselves who now number almost one hundred. These men, who come mainly from simple backgrounds, not only perform needed services but also receive the chance for education and personal development usually available only to India's upper classes.

The brothers all welcomed me into their home and periodically have asked to hear stories of the "old days." Yes, they still ask for the Monkey Bite Story. Private conversations, periodic reminiscences, and zipping through the streets clinging to the back of a motorbike to see the brothers' works have filled my days—and, oh yes, those lattes at Café Coffee Day on M.G. Road.

Wellness note: I am just fine, though I did succumb to the three-day flu that has floored half of Bangalore. India has ordinary ills as well as acute ones. So I lost several days because of it, but gained back the time philosophizing how impossible it is to "lose" days. I'm sure you can see that too much self-reflection is a quick slide down the chute into the loony bin.

I went to the pharmacy the other day to purchase Valium. I had no prescription but it's fairly easy to get whatever you want over the counter in India.

Why did I want Valium? I wasn't particularly stressed but, although Valium is used to decrease anxiety, physiologically it is a muscle relaxant. Because I had experienced a severe muscle cramp in my leg about three months ago in the U.S.—that lasted for several days in spite of all the usual tricks—I figured it would be useful to have a cache of V's on hand. And where else to get it without any hassle but in India?

When the teenage clerk asked me how many I wanted, I thought I'd go big and ask for twenty.

"Twenty strips? No problem."

"Uh, how many are on a strip?"

When he said "ten" and I realized he was about to send me out the door with 200 Valium tablets, I paused. What about U.S. customs? I settled on two strips and headed back to the brothers' house for my final evening there, the V's tingling in my pocket.

The City of Angels and the Stone Tablets

What a mistake. Now I'll have to eat my words.

I had told both faculty and students at the massage school where I teach that I would be taking additional training in Thai massage at its very home, a monastery in old Bangkok. I had imagined that later I'd sail into my Thai massage classes in California and mention ever so casually, "My teacher at the monastery in Bangkok showed that move this way you see."

Usually I'm fairly practical so I don't know what possessed me to think that at the end of five weeks of travel in Asia that I would be up for attending classes seven hours a day. So, too pooped to push and pull someone else's limbs, I settled for the next best thing: receiving many, many Thai massages. I am learning by feel.

Thai massage in a monastery? Thai massage actually has its origins in India with Buddhist monks to whom were entrusted not only spiritual duties but also health care for the people. As Buddhism migrated to Thailand in the safekeeping of the monks, so did traditional medicine. That medicine included both herbal remedies and massage, and because of its monastic foundations, certain protocols were stated.

These rules are still found in the literature today. Prayer before each session—currently practiced at least as a personal "centering" time. Not doing massage in the market place—unseemly for monks but no longer an absolute for lay practitioners. Not accepting money since monks were not even to touch money—clearly not followed by today's practitioners. These standards are mentioned to help students set a "tone" for the work, and to some extent this has been successful.

Several hundred years ago many of the ancient massage texts with both practical and theoretical information about Thai massage were destroyed by Khmers from the east invading Thailand. One of Siam's kings later ordered that the basic foundations of Thai medicine and massage—the "energy paths" running throughout the body, or *sen* lines—be engraved on slate tablets and preserved at Wat Pho, the premier monastery (*wat* means monastery) of Krung Thep. Krung Thep, or The City of Angels, is what we now call plain old Bangkok. I'm reminded that plain old LA is really The City of Our Lady of The Angels.

One goal for me on this journey was to see those stone carvings, which I had often spoken about in my Thai massage classes. I studied the maps of the 20-acre monastery, asked the guides and scoured the temples, to no avail. As in trying to find Vulture's Peak of Buddhist interest, no one seemed to know what I was talking about. The solution to locating the engravings sprang into my mind on my second day. Seek out an American student at the massage training center in the monastery. Debbie from Montana referred me to John from Florida who told me in a very Thai way that the carvings were in a cloister "at the feet of the Reclining Buddha."

And there they were. I had first paid my respects to the 140-foot long Reclining Buddha, whose small toenail is twice the size of my torso, then approached the unimposing structure that was my destination. The engravings, smaller than I had imagined—just 2.5 feet high and tucked up under the eaves, maybe 60–70 of them—were nevertheless touching to see. A sought-after symbol of my own convictions—that our bodies are more than "matter"—had been found in a distant land where ancient Indian, Buddhist, and Thai practices accorded primacy and sacred importance to the "energy body."

The pictures, born of experience and placed in the small building a few paces from the pavilion where massage is ministered daily, essentially map out the energy flows throughout the body, similar to but not the same as Chinese meridians. Accurate or not, the images attest to the traditional practice of recognizing the role of "energy" in healing work. I sat and stared contentedly at them for a long time as noisy tour groups passed by.

On pilgrimage: Clearly one of the delights of the pilgrim is to finally experience places read and heard about—like the stone tablets—yet this must be balanced by the readiness for the unexpected event that contains charm or a lesson for our soul. For example, the missed train that created the dazzling trip through the Haridwar bazaar at twilight, and which had earlier that day pushed me to learn a bit more patience as I waited in Delhi for the later train. Or the three-day flu in Bangalore that slowed me down to spend unrushed time with the brothers.

How to do this? Leave enough space in your schedule and it will happen. Don't leave enough space and it will likely happen anyway though you may stress more over it. The mythologist Joseph Campbell once said, "We must be willing to let go of the life we planned so as to have the life that is waiting for us."

Ninja Masseuse

IF YOUR IMAGE of Thai massage is that of being pushed, pulled, pummeled, pounded, prodded, poked, and paddled, you are partially correct. But it feels really good—most of the time.

Thai massage can be thought of as having three main components: thumb pressure along the energy lines, called "point work," solid pressure over muscles using the hand or foot, and stretches. In the U.S., we teach the "point work" in a slow, gentle fashion. Not so the style of the petite women in Bangkok. Woe to the hypersensitive client who falls into the hands of those ninja masseuses at Wat Pho who nevertheless smile continually as they ply their craft.

Solid pressure needs no explanation, but the stretches have a curious history. In Wat Pho, established primarily as a medical monastery, one can find the Hill of the Contorted Hermits. The stone statues—only 24 of 80 still remain—show the figures in various pretzel positions, originally yogic poses that had come to be used for self-cure of multiple diseases. These poses found their way into Thai medical massage as the highly creative stretches you may have seen. So, you want to practice yoga but are too lazy? Get a Thai massage session and have someone do it for you. Naturally my rates will go up after having imbibed at The Source.

The Thai people. I've not said much about these (otherwise) gentle, courteous folk. Intense traffic pervades Bangkok yet there is no incessant honking of horns—they wait. Streets are clean of garbage and hardly a beggar shows his face. Yes, shopkeepers bark their wares but one need only to smile and say "no" once. And the Thais are genuinely friendly.

The other evening I was caught in a downpour while heading back to my hotel. At the gate of another hotel along the way, the night watchman waved me over to join him under his umbrella, a welcoming grin on his face. When I finally entered my own ice-cold air-conditioned hotel lobby soaking wet, my teeth chattered as I asked for my key. Two girls at the desk shouted to a third: "Quick, quick, key for Mistah James. He sooo coooold."

It must be acknowledged: Bangkok is the sex capital of Asia. Whole busloads of Japanese businessmen traverse the town on scheduled sex tours, and nightclubs abound where Thai ladies—I am told—perform amazing feats with ping pong balls and Coke bottles. The history of the modern sex industry in Bangkok goes back to its role as a major Rest and Recreation destination for American soldiers serving in Vietnam.

The hotel I am staying in was in fact hastily erected in the 60s to accommodate such excursions. Soldiers have traditionally employed sex, consensual or not, to blot out the horrors they have seen or have perpetrated themselves, as well as the concomitant shame of participating in those actions. A persistent but likely not accurate version of ancient temple prostitutes has them "tending to" combatants returning from war to help the men reenter society and find their own nurturing side. Even if totally a myth, the story is an indication of our deep understanding that war/death and sex are first cousins, if not siblings.

As per good business practices, my hotel has diversified and now both female and male potential companions discreetly lounge in the lobby (lobby in the lounge?). For those of you wishing the X-rated version of this email, you'll just have to wheedle it out of me some night over a glass, uh bottle, of wine. Well, maybe one story.

The Prince and I
There was that time in the 80s that I met a member of the Thai royal family at a gay bar.

At Harry's Bar in Bangkok, I found myself in conversation with a gregarious young Thai man who said his name was "Nut." A slim, yet athletic-looking man—a kick-boxer by profession it turned out—he seemed to know most people there and smiled generously at everyone. When another man came up to greet Nut, it was clear they were old friends though the newcomer appeared to be on the quiet side. After exchanging quick greetings with him in Thai, Nut turned to me and introduced his friend.

"This is Dara but he doesn't come here much. I have to beg him. We are having luck tonight."

"I'm very pleased to meet you, Jim, and I hope you're having a good experience in our country. Let me know how I might assist you. It would be my pleasure."

Dara, of average height and sporting a warm smile, was soft-spoken though his command of English suggested he was highly educated. He also exuded an easy air of confidence that was intriguing in itself.

We chatted a few more moments about where I was staying, what sights I must take in, whether or not I was going to the ocean.

"You should really see the ancient capital, Ayutthaya. It's not far from the city and more interesting than a bar," Dara said.

In a stage whisper Nut explained that Dara didn't like the bar scene much since he was a member of the royal family. Dara brushed off the comment about being royal, but I asked, "Are you serious? Or are you kidding me?"

"It's true. I'll show you," Dara said. "Nut, we'll pick you up in the morning for Ayutthaya."

Dara drove me to the legendary Oriental Hotel to see pictures of the royal family on its lobby walls. In one photo he pointed out his grandfather, one of the eighty-four offspring of King Mongkut, or Rama IV. The man had thirty-two wives. Mongkut was portrayed in the play and film *The King and I*, which according to Dara had *not* been well-received in Thailand. Mongkut was highly intelligent and spoke nearly perfect English, bearing almost no resemblance to the movie caricature of him.

Dara showed me his royal passport with diplomatic immunity, and explained the "royalty" situation. In order that the country not be overrun by royals due to their exponential increase in numbers, only those who were a direct descendant of the current ruling king would always be royals. All others would cease to be "royal" after the fourth generation. Dara was the last of his line.

At Ayutthaya the next day, we three walked the grounds—ruins of ancient monasteries and palaces, rows of Buddha statutes, serene ponds—while Dara held my hand most of the time as Asian men often do. With sideways glances at him, I started to think that "My prince has come." I was beginning to really like Dara, and images abounded in my mind of invitations to royal parties, preferred seating at events, being part of an "in crowd." My, how those at home would be envious of me when I relayed all that no doubt would follow this casual outing.

After a leisurely lunch we headed back to Bangkok—and the day came to an end with fond farewells, but nothing more.

While I had let my fantasies carry me away, I like to think that I was not blind to the wonderful reality of that day. My fertile imagination and hopeful expectations happily did not totally distract me from experiencing what was present in front of me. I wasn't on a tour bus with twenty other Westerners—I had spent the day with two engaging local people who treated me as a friend. What more could I want?

The conclusion to my stay in Bangkok: for $7, an hour-long foot and leg massage. Now, *that's* pleasure.

Giving Massage as a Vehicle for Inner Work

MASSAGE IS A delight to receive and in many cases a modality for healing. For me it has, additionally, had a significant and impactful role on my inner life.

Upon returning to the U.S. in 1986 after living on the Indian Subcontinent for seven years, I wanted to retool myself for a new vocation. I had no idea what that might be, and while I had found teaching math to be satisfying in my younger days, I had no desire to return to that profession.

A friend, and former fellow-pioneer of the India/Nepal project, was studying "holistic health" in the San Francisco Bay Area at the time. We talked one day, and he had advice for me.

"After all those years in India, you're likely worn out. Focus on your own physical wellbeing for now," Joe said. "I know of a massage program here in the Bay Area you'd probably enjoy."

I thought, oh well, that would be a nice three-week adjunct to whatever other classes I'll take during my sabbatical. At the time I had no idea that those few weeks would lead to further massage training and an enjoyable, stimulating, and wonderful career of nearly thirty years. How that one offhand (accidental?) suggestion ended up shaping so much of my life!

From math to massage—from the cerebral to the sensate. What a satisfying, integrating journey it has been.

A small book would be required to relate all that I learned by participating in that field of endeavor, so I shall mention only two items.

First, I gradually was able to withdraw my judgments of another person based on the condition or status of their body. Yes, I periodically did think to myself, "He's quite overweight and that's not healthy. He should do something about it. Why hasn't he?" "If she would pay more attention to nutrition and exercise she wouldn't complain about constant lack of energy. Doesn't she have any self-discipline?" Slowly, however, as I came to know these individuals and heard some of their stories, I examined my attitude. I stepped back from such judgment and, most importantly, somehow I reached the point where I didn't need to know someone's backstory to have compassion for them.

Compassion doesn't require understanding. It is simply an attitude and habit of the mind and heart that we first extend to ourselves, and then to others.

Second, I learned at a depth that I had never understood before to be "truly present" to the person in front of me. While I like to think I developed that attitude with each client, no clients were more my teachers in that matter than those who were sick or dying.

My Hands Have Memory

ONE DAY, A soft-spoken man hesitantly spoke on the phone.

"Do you massage people with AIDS?"

It broke my heart that he felt he needed to ask but I suppose he had received rejections in various ways already. We booked an appointment and I gave him my address.

Chris saw me for several sessions. An artist and sensitive soul, this beautiful young man with a once nearly perfect body said little as we worked together. His sad eyes spoke more than his words. He lay on my massage table, his body racked by an invader, and seemed to have complete trust in me and my touch. I have seldom been in the presence of someone I had so, so wanted to hold and "will" his disease away.

That did not, could not, happen. But I was forced to be totally present as my hands massaged his fragile body. I could not let myself think of my shopping list or anything else so trivial in comparison to that man's life.

I would gauge his response to my touch not only by verbal comments he gave but also by the slight reactions of his body. He might retract ever so slightly from my hands, which I interpreted as my pressure being too heavy or that he was "finished" with massage for the day. He could absorb only so much. Sometimes, though, he would lean into my hands, seemingly to feel my touch more fully.

When Chris was no longer physically able to come to my place or afford payment, I went to the hospice where he was then staying to give him massage. But he was getting thinner and weaker and his bones became more prominent. Each week I could literally feel the continued wasting of his body.

And one day he was gone.

It seems that my hands have memory. And while that can help me assess muscle development, it also means I am pulled onto the path of another person's dying process. A path not possible to tread lightly.

While I had several private clients like Chris with life-threatening illnesses, I also immersed myself into such care by volunteering as a massage therapist at the AIDS Center in Oakland. Over seven years, I met men in all stages of the disease and was pushed ever more and more into a space of non-judgment and total presence.

I remember a man, John, who always said, "See you next time, Jim," at the end of his session. One day he whispered only, "Goodbye." I never saw him again for he died the following week. He knew.

I am indebted to each of these men for allowing me to touch them, and to further my own inner work.

A New Age Sabbatical

MASSAGE AND OTHER training filled my sabbatical time after India, but first I had had to be clear with myself and my religious superiors that I wasn't going to have the usual type of sabbatical the brothers took at that time, or like the academically oriented ones I'd had in the past.

In October 1957, the Soviets launched the earth's first artificial satellite—Sputnik. This small metal sphere less than two feet in diameter changed the world. The space race was on. The shocked American scientific community wrung its hands and decided America needed to ramp up its proficiency in science and math, and the recently created National Science Foundation would be the vehicle for that. The NSF provided grants to math and science teachers for graduate work, figuring that that effort would trickle down to better-prepared students and future scientists.

I applied for such a grant and was soon spending four summers in Ohio in the 60s pursuing a master's in math.

Those studies afforded me mainly two benefits: I *finally* understood calculus (I think)—a feat I was unsure I'd ever accomplish—and my ego was fluffed by having extra initials behind my name. I don't remember much else of those sum-mers other than reading gothic romance novels—set along the windy cliffs of Cornwall—in an effort to give my brain a rest from the hieroglyphics of subjects like topology.

In the 70s the brother in charge of personnel for all the brothers' schools approached me about studying educational administration, and I agreed. I was nearing ten years of teach-ing high school mathematics and began wondering, "Is this all there is?" Maybe administration was my next step. While those studies on a beautiful campus in California were more enlivening than the math courses, the daily drudge of high school administration itself was a deadening weight on my soul. I felt I was daily struggling for air to breathe and mainly going through the motions of my duties. I had no heart for the work. That surprised me as well as others, since we all had thought I would be good at administration.

It turned out that I possessed administrative skills but high school was the wrong venue. Mine were "big picture" skills: planning, putting new structures in place, pioneering new projects, engaging key players in a cooperative effort, cre-ating a vision for the future. The India project was where I caught my administrative stride.

At one level, that mission engaged my adventurous side, and I was quite capable of riding overnight trains, dealing with robbery or changing visa rules, and seeking solutions that others had not yet considered. And as the Director of that effort, not only did I interact with government and church officials, but the program itself was something that I and my team started "from scratch." My job involved three different countries directly and another two peripherally. I was, as they say, "in my element" in India.

But what now, in my post-India period? I had been advised by my religious superiors that taking classes in "theological renewal" would be a good idea during my sabbatical. I responded—I'm afraid in a rather smarmy way—that, "Theology needs renewal, not me." But those superiors had visited India and Nepal, seen the challenges involved in that project, and even gotten sick while there. I suspect they might have approved a semester on the beaches of Hawaii had I pressed for it. And so they agreed to my sabbatical plan, which included not only massage education but living in a Berkeley apartment close to the richness of the classes and workshops available in that city.

Two courses, besides massage, offered in Berkeley that caught my attention were about dreams.

I had always been fascinated by dreams, those nightly visitations of improbable narratives peopled by characters not always recognizable or clearly remembered in morning light. I hadn't, however, read or studied about dreams. I just let what I could remember of them dance in my mind after waking.

The first piece of dream work I did many years earlier, therefore, seemed a fluke, an accident.

As a high school instructor, I and a number of other teachers from several schools had run a "leadership camp" at the end of summer for juniors going into their senior year. We staff bonded closely so it was no surprise that one day at our planning meeting, a member said he was troubled by a dream from the previous night.

"Tell us," we all said.

"All I can remember is that I was in a forest, choking a young deer."

Silence in the group.

The one thing about dreams I had heard from a psychotherapist friend was that everything in the dream was a part of the dreamer. So I questioned him.

"What words come to your mind when you think of a young deer?"

Tender, sweet, loving, he said. Eventually he realized he was choking off his *own* tender, loving feelings toward someone. His face lit up with recognition, and I was sold on dream work. The major benefit of dream work, it seems, is to bring to consciousness that which is unconscious. Then we can be proactive about what is happening in our soul, rather than let "it" drag us hither and thither.

During the spring of my unsatisfying high school administration year, I had a dream in which I was at my office desk, simultaneously talking to someone on the phone, typing a letter, and listening to the complaints of a school counselor who sat across from me. But I already knew I felt overloaded with duties. The key to new information in the dream was that instead of sitting on my swivel desk chair I was sitting on a commode, defecating explosively.

My conscious mind had been bent on continuing the job I was trained for, but my unconscious told me how I really felt about it: s#*t on this job. I quit at the end of that school year.

Toward the conclusion of my stay in India/Nepal, I had a dream of giving birth to a baby. Don't ask me how, I don't know. The gestation period was over, new life had emerged. I could nurture it a bit longer, then move on. And I did.

In Berkeley I discovered two well-known dream experts who mentored me in dream work, and one of them eventually asked me to co-facilitate dream groups with him. During those group sessions, I found I was doing my own internal work while offering projections on another person's dream, and simultaneously providing others a vehicle for their inner work. The dream work path to awareness and guidance has proved invaluable to me over the years and remains dear to my heart.

This I have learned: *To look deeply into our dreams is to do soul work at perhaps its most primal and universally experienced manifestation of all.*

I also met my first boyfriend that sabbatical year while, yes, still a brother.

It was 1986 and my 45th birthday in late August. Expecting to just pass the time before I took myself out to dinner, I strolled along the shore of the Bay and came upon a young man in shorts and T-shirt lying on a blanket.

As I neared him, he said "Hi" and asked me what I was doing. I replied, "Just walking," and asked him what he was doing.

"Trying to get a sun tan," he said, and laughed at his own joke. He was an African-American man.

Seventeen years my junior and a flight attendant, M soon became a regular companion, and certainly didn't complain when I wanted to practice massage on him. When he learned my story, especially the part about being just "off the boat" from Asia, he made it his mission to show me around town and have me dress properly.

"You're kidding. You cannot go out wearing *that*. We're going to Macy's."

I also got a tiny glimpse of the lot of minorities in our land. It wasn't unusual for the greeter at a department store or restaurant to direct their welcome clearly at me rather than the both of us. M was gracious, but now and then might say archly, "Oh, don't I get a greeting?"

While the "boyfriend" mode did not last, M and I remained friends over the years. It seems that often happens with gay men. Why not stay friends with someone who knows you and with whom you have been intimate? And there is that bittersweet saying, "Friends last longer than lovers."

Almost Paradise

ABOUT A HALF-DAY'S train ride or a short plane flight south of Bangkok lie some of the world's most pristine beaches and islands. Names like Koh Samui conjure images of Bali Hai, and travelers I know as well as strangers I've met have labeled them Paradise.

I didn't go there. Instead, I opted for the glitzy, commercialized resort town of Pattaya just two hours from Bangkok. Why? Mainly because it is indeed a "short" taxi ride from this beach town directly back to the Bangkok airport, and it has what I want: ocean, sea breezes, excellent hotels and restaurants, and an oceanside promenade where every manner of tourist and Thai strolls at dusk.

Over the years I have learned the wisdom of ending an interesting, though very likely hectic, trip in Asia with "down" time in a relaxing location. This insight has served me well, and others I have passed it on to agree as well. Pattaya is my current antidote to travel stress.

I have also discovered the importance of finding "my spot" in any locale I visit, and from that vantage point most conditions less desirable fade away, such as noise, dust, and crowds. One of my spots in Pattaya is my hotel itself.

An "older" hotel set on a secluded half-acre of palm trees, its front gate is just 50 feet from the ocean and the promenade. It also sports a 90-foot pool where I swim each morning upon rising. All this for $35 a night, including the overwhelming breakfast buffet.

The hotel is frequented by a variety of travelers, though the biggest single group is the German seniors who chain smoke. They are everywhere here. Signs in the hotel are in that language as well as the usual Thai and English, and there is even a German restaurant under the palms here, the Zeppelin, which offers heavy meals of roast pork and dumplings with thick gravy. In the tropics? No wonder they—the well-rounded Germans—slug around the pool all day and seem to require great effort to lift their beer steins.

A French guy I met at the beach yesterday asked me how did I, a non-retiree, get so much vacation time. Europeans apparently know the American work machine. I didn't "get" it, I took it—unpaid. Studies show that Europeans get as much as four times the paid vacation as Americans, yet their economies are *no less productive*. In the U.S. our output is diminished by stress-related time off from work, on-the-job injuries, and absenteeism due mainly to alcoholism. State Disability funds have paid for many an unplanned "vacation." Why wait?

And so, Gentle Readers, the days here at oceanside pass. Walks along the beach, a boat trip to Pearl Island, reading, writing, swimming, chatting with other travelers over lunch—these activities fill my day. I make forays into the food bazaars where chicken kabobs grill on live coals next to freshly caught shrimp, and immense clay bowls hold fluorescent-colored noodles in milk. Soup simmers in caldrons and pre-packaged portions sit in small clear plastic bags on the counter, much like the goldfish bag you carried home from the pet store.

I half-hope that my uneventful days will make me desirous of leaping back into classes, meetings, and computer projects. I don't think the ploy is working.

And now at the passing of the full moon, this night when Thai people cast small flower boats on rivers, streams, the ocean, and all bodies of water that sustain their lives—Loy Kra Thong Festival—the journey has come to an end. This pilgrim's feet are weary and must rest. What has it been all about? Yes, I have gone to several holy places as the tarot card suggested—or more accurately, as per what I read into that card—and occasionally used frustration to stare more directly at the demands of my own ego. But how have I changed or grown?

I'd like to think that simply by walking amid so many others less fortunate than myself, I have deepened my capacity for compassion. The impromptu encounters with both fellow travelers and local people have helped me see an interesting soul, with their own joys and sorrows, in every single person. Startling scenery has reawakened my sense of awe. And running through all those attitudes is a deep feeling of gratitude for life itself.

Nevertheless, the rational side of my being wants to come up with the Great Insight that will endure when the suntan fades and the memories dim. I could indeed write more at this point, falsely confident that in a plethora of words lurks the unsaid perception which will further enlighten my world. But I choose not to. The lesson of the Flower Sermon—that the greatest truths cannot be put into words—goes with me like an angel perched on my shoulder, whispering in my ear should I need a reminder.

I also know that if there is an important insight from these travels that hasn't yet been grasped, it will come to me after I reach home, in that casual moment of stepping off the curb or placing my coffee cup down, or after freshly awakening from that Magic Mirror that never lies—the world of dreams.

2006

Nepal, Thailand, Philippines

Curfew

Kathmandu, Nepal
February 2006

HAPPILY I DIDN'T know that "Shoot to kill" were the orders given to the Nepali army—later confirmed by the U.S. Embassy—for anyone on Kathmandu streets after the 11 p.m. curfew. The Maoist rebellion had reached the capital and security was high.

My flight to Kathmandu which was to arrive nicely at 9 p.m. naturally landed at 12:30 a.m. Royal Nepal Airlines informed us we could either stay in the frigid airport until 5 a.m. or take their bus to the nearby Everest Hotel where we'd wait out the curfew in their lobby. They omitted the information about the army's orders and we all jumped on the bus.

Three times along our two-mile route, surly looking soldiers toting rifles and seemingly eager to show their power (in the past, even ambulances approaching a hospital had been fired upon) flagged us down, examined our driver's papers, and grimly waved us on with their weapons—their fingers still curled around the trigger.

Inside the Everest Sheraton Hotel, comfy sofas and over-stuffed chairs welcomed our bones, but our ears were assaulted for the next five hours by Nepali travelers joining with the hotel waiters and the lobby manager attempting to pass the time by belting out folk tunes from childhood.

The chilly winter air we had inhaled along the way to the hotel reminded me of my own move to Kathmandu in January 1982. Pervasive cold in the Himalayas at 4500 feet. And dark. At the time, electricity was available only on alternate nights in the nation's capital, so we bundled ourselves in blankets and headed for bed by 9 at night. The only home I ever visited that sported central heating and consistent electricity was the U.S. ambassador's home. The rest of us made do with candles and weak electric space heaters or smelly kerosene heaters. No wonder that now was the first time I had returned to visit Kathmandu friends in the winter.

But I was already on the Indian subcontinent for another reason.

* * *

It was in 1980 that three other brothers and I had traveled to India to start a branch of our religious order there. The year 2005 was thus the 25th Jubilee Year, culminating with celebrations in December 2005 and January 2006 in Bangalore, South India.

The invitation to the celebration had arrived from India in early 2005 and I was very touched and pleased to be included. In "days of old" a former member of a religious order (an "ex") would not have been invited to such a celebration and given the warm welcome and honors as I was. In the *really* old days, the letter from Rome giving dispensation from one's vows began with, "Dear unfaithful son."

Fortunately, a new era and attitude in religious orders was promoting an appreciation of the contributions of everyone, whether currently members or not. By circumstance, I was the only one of the original Four—some called us the Gang of Four in 1980—present at the jubilee event.

Returning to India for this celebration was another "pilgrimage," one to my Christian and Catholic roots this time. I would be immersed in that culture for a few weeks, see old friends, and then bid that world adieu.

At the end of the celebration, I had journeyed eastward to the beaches of the Coromandel Coast of India to relax, and ponder. And with a full heart, I concluded that while I would still maintain individual friendships with many brothers, I had now finally closed the "Brothers in India" chapter of my life. It had been a challenging and soul-stirring period in my life, a time that moved me forward and deeper, and one that I was now letting go of.

* * *

Who Am I?

It was also time for me to let go of identifying—albeit less and less—as a "former brother." Though I had officially left the Brotherhood nearly twenty years earlier, and was now leaving behind my connection with the Indian part of that lifestyle, the "identity" of "former brother" somehow wanted to claim me. Is there no end to this latching onto roles we play in life?

True, the lessons learned and habits developed over nearly thirty years as a brother would remain with me. And I wanted that. I had grown much during that time, and hoped to keep in my soul the practice of being open to the "transcendent" in life, an attitude that the life of a brother had encouraged. And the habit of taking time on a daily basis for reflection, or meditation, or deep pondering—call it what you will—serves me to this day. But still. How to avoid getting caught in the cloying web of identification with the new "role of the moment"?

Wise writers on this subject tell us to "become an observer" and step back from whatever role we currently have. Watch ourselves and our activities as from a distance. When this becomes more of a habit than an occasional exercise, we shall be able to gain insight into our true nature.

Or perhaps go a bit nuts? I remember several times as a young child lying in my bed of an afternoon, looking out my window at the apple tree in our side yard and trying to understand, "Who is Jimmy?" I really did aim to "step back" from myself, though I didn't know those terms at the time. I even wondered if "Jimmy" would continue to function if "I" forgot about him.

At a certain point during those musings, I would invariably feel like I was falling through space—floating at first, then falling, falling, into an unknown abyss. I finally stopped the practice fearing that I could lose my mind. A Zen teacher might say, "Go ahead, lose your mind. Go for no-mind." But my six or seven-year-old psyche couldn't handle it—certainly not on my own without guidance.

I used to think it rather harsh to send those small boys off to Buddhist monasteries at age six or so, but now I view it rather differently. Perhaps all youngsters have those semi-mystical moments of wondering who they really are, and coaching from elders in that metaphysical realm would be good for the soul and a great start to a lifetime of self-reflection.

However, I would promote a "day camp" type of monastery experience and let those bouncy boys go back to their mothers and fathers at the end of the day where they belong.

For now, my intention shall be to move toward the "observer" stance in daily life: to see myself now as a traveler, now as a long-time friend, now as a sad or happy person, now as...

* * *

Back to my arrival in Kathmandu amidst men with guns.

Comfortably safe a few hours later in the apartment of my old friend Greg, an American Jesuit, I got the whole political story.

In 1996 the Communist Party of Nepal, or Maoists, launched a rebellion with the express aim of overthrowing the monarchy and establishing a People's Republic. The constitutional monarchy, agreed to and supported by King Birendra in 1990, was not acceptable to them because it hadn't gone far enough.

The current king, Gyanendra, had ascended the throne after the death of his brother King Birendra in the massacre at the palace in June 2001 and the demise of his nephew Prince Dipendra three days later. Dipendra, the Crown Prince, was the perpetrator of the massacre but nevertheless was king by right of succession upon the death of his father. He had, however, suffered a self-inflicted wound the night of his rampage which subsequently led to his death, after having been king for only a few days—and in a coma.

King Gyanendra had hoped to bring the country to order. But following the failure of the government to hold needed elections and coax the rebels to the negotiating table, he dismissed his prime minister and took over as absolute ruler in February 2005. He promised that Nepal would have "peace and effective democracy" within three years but his actions were met with much opposition. Both the people and the political parties felt it was too far to the "right" from the constitutional monarchy that had existed earlier.

The Maoists had called a unilateral ceasefire some months ago, but King Gyanendra had moved to a harder position. With apparently no budging on the palace's side, the Maoists turned once again to shootings and burning police stations. The shock this time was that recently several such incidents occurred in Kathmandu Valley itself, a rare tactic.

Each day the evening curfew has been moved up—tonight rumor has it that the curfew is 8 p.m. Meanwhile, from my lodgings here in the Thamel section of Kathmandu, I make forays to visit old friends and shop for a few items. A local friend, Dinesh, races me around the city on his motorcycle. Yes, I wear a helmet.

Tomorrow, Greg, I, and Chandra—Greg's cook and friend, who has a B.A. in English but gets better pay as Greg's cook than somehow using his degree—are scheduled to fly down to Pokhara for a three-day vacationette. I bought their tickets as a hospitality "thank you." Also planned for tomorrow is a political protest which the palace is attempting to crush by a means of a city-wide imposed strike. All shops are to be closed, no vehicles on the street. We could walk the few miles to the airport, but the real challenge would be if the other rumor is true of an actual daytime curfew and we couldn't go out at all. But that is rumor at this point.

Escape to Pokhara

OUR TAXI SPED through Kathmandu's narrow streets at 7:30 a.m. in a determined effort to reach the airport before the 8 a.m. daytime curfew. People rushed to buy food, get some place else, or seemingly just to be frantic. Even though the army's orders were still "Shoot to kill," during the daytime curfew, I didn't see any soldiers on the street except at the airport, our very destination.

To thwart today's peaceful protest—by a coalition of seven political parties against the palace's running of the country—the curfew had been ordered, the leaders of all the opposing parties put under house arrest, and the transmission towers for mobile phones all disabled. You might know that in countries like Nepal, many urban dwellers have mobile phones which generally are more dependable than a weak or broken infrastructure of land lines. So, there could be no organizing of alternate protest plans via mobile phones.

At the airport, frenzy was the order of the day. However, since any number of graduates of St. Xavier's, the local Jesuit school, are airline agents and would do anything to assist Father Greg, by 8:45 a.m. we three lifted off in an 18-passenger aircraft instead of our scheduled 1 p.m. departure. I believe I can still navigate

India and Nepal myself, but it's wonderful to be taken care of now and then.

Nepal's airline names are reminiscent of hippie dreams: Buddha Air (our flight), Yeti Air (just who/what is flying this thing?), Gorkha Air (makes you feel safe), and Cosmic Air (my favorite name). In India, my favorite name was Spice Air, though I also liked Kingfisher Airlines. That name is an Indian brewery's flagship brand, and it would be like having a Bud Lite Airlines. (Did the pilots take a breath test?)

Today, relaxed at our hotel in Pokhara only a few yards from Phewa Lake and enjoying morning coffee on the verandah while the others still sleep, I am watching life flow past. Three vegetable vendors have already wheeled their carts down the street. Why not have fresh vegetables brought to your door rather than trudging to the market?

A few of you may remember when the Milk Man personally delivered his goods to your porch and the Bread Man also appeared at your door. In Milwaukee, our bread guy was the "Omar Man" though we seldom called him that. "Mom, the Bread Man is here," we kids would call out as his van snaked down our curved driveway. We also had an Egg Lady, though we went to her house ourselves, just up the street in our semi-rural neighborhood, to collect freshly laid eggs.

Next door was the Pigeon Man, not because we bought pigeons from him but because he had a pigeon coop right at the edge of our property. I never understood what he used the pigeons for. He seldom said much, not even when he returned an arrow to me that had lodged in his roof after I tried to shoot a pigeon with my new bow-and-arrow set. Though I was young, I was properly embarrassed.

The veggie vendor here in Pokhara has no cool van to tool around town in. His cart is a flat board, perhaps three by five feet, mounted on four patched bicycle tires. And no fancy axles that allow for easy turns. He has to pick up one end of the cart to direct the vehicle into the side lane. Never mind that signs all over Pokhara say in Nepali, "No pushcarts on the street."

Just as my spirit was settling into the slow pace of life in this lakeside town, dozens of motorcycles bearing political party banners broke the calm and roared past my coffee spot. Groups of people on both sides of the road either cheered or booed as a particular group went past. A few men shook their fist at one contingent, a group I found out later that was loyal to the monarch. The country is in agitation everywhere.

Tomorrow I will be going to visit Ram's wife and daughters.

Ram's Family

RAM, YOU MAY recall, was a porter/companion on my Anna-purna trek some 20 or so years ago. His career in the police force was interrupted by the revolutionary Maoists who saw police as instruments of the corrupt monarchical institution. Conse-quently, his life had been threatened, his family harassed, and his sister-in-law beaten with a lead pipe last year when she wouldn't tell the Maoists where he was at the time (hiding in the labyrin-thine bazaar).

With Greg's help and international contacts, he managed to get out of the country. He now works in the Middle East though his family has spread the rumor that he has gone to India. On the home front, his wife works as a pre-kindergarten teacher and looks after the girls. Several friends in the U.S. and I have been supporting the daughters' education in a local private school of a much better quality than the government school.

Greg and I visited Ram's wife, Urmila, and the girls: Neha, 14, and Rosie, 12. They live in a simple but solid clay house consisting of three separate rooms running along a verandah, and a corrugated metal roof above—held in place during the monsoons by large rocks. Four years ago, all rooms opened only onto the verandah, the sole way to get from one room to the other—a traditional Nepali home in Pokhara. Now, to prevent any untoward acts perpetrated after dark, the rooms are connected on the inside.

I brought a shawl for Urmila and trendy little backpacks filled with games for the girls. We played Chinese Checkers (heaven knows if I taught them the standard rules of that game from my long-ago childhood) and had fun with the "Science Quiz" game (in English, bought in Kathmandu). Neha and Rosie are quite bright, and laughed when they saw me peeking at the answers for myself. I did that *only* to show that nobody has to know all the answers...

On another visit, Urmila served a dinner of delicious curried chicken and rice. Cardamom and turmeric scents swirled in the air and pulled from the well of my mind memories of familiar Asian nourishment and genuine hospitality.

We also spent time looking at the astrological charts for each of them and Ram. In Nepal, these are traditionally drawn up within the first month of a child's birth and given to them on a scroll. As you unroll the scroll, you touch the fingers of your right hand to the scroll, then to your forehead to show respect. Ram's and Urmila's were hand written on cloth, with the twelve "houses" of the chart represented by twelve lotus petals.

I had studied the basics of astrology, so when Greg refreshed my memory of the Devanagari script—the alphabet used for Hindi, Nepali, and several other languages as well—I could identify *surya*, Sun, and *chandrama*, Moon, the most important "planets" in astrology. The particular area of the birth chart they appear in gives clues as to what themes might play out in the person's life.

All were amazed at how, especially for Ram and Urmila, the patterns I described had already been playing out. Ram's chart indicated that in terms of work, he would likely choose some-thing of service to others. His years as a policeman confirmed that. He also had the planet of abundance, Jupiter, in an area that suggested he would be quite social and have lots of friends. "Yes, yes," they clapped. "What else?"

How wonderful to have some sense of astrology which is not only intercultural, but in this case, highly revered by Nepalis. They now think I am some kind of *jhankari*, shaman, as well as Good Guy from California where the streets, they know, are paved with gold.

If It's in Your Stars, It's in Your Soul

AS A CHILD, I must have looked dozens of times at the collection of postcards tucked away in the top drawer of the dresser in our extra bedroom. Oddly, I can remember only one postcard—that of the Grand Coulee Dam, somewhere so far from Milwaukee it might as well have been a foreign country. Was it that periodic ritual that engendered in me a desire to travel? At the time I thought everybody felt that way. But no, many folks are content with the familiar, their "usual" environment—even though unexpected events and challenges nevertheless spur their lives forward in that setting—and they are the better for it.

While they learn life's lessons in their customary settings, I seem to have required the conspiracy of other cultures, ones quite frustrating though fascinating, to move my life forward and deeper.

There are indications in my astrological chart which can explain that propensity of mine but first, a word about astrology.

I don't "believe" in astrology. In fact, I have no use for "belief" in the traditional sense of taking *any* "authority's" word about unseen realities. We need only a quick look at history to see the suffering caused when people blindly accept one set of beliefs and deem another group's beliefs deserving of being stamped out.

So, I do not take anyone's word about whether astrology is "true" or not. I only look at whether examining my personal astrological configurations can help me grow in awareness. This is the same approach I take with the various paradigms of "personality," such as the Enneagram and Jungian typologies. If these systems regularly shed a ray of light on our lives and help us understand ourselves better, then let's employ them.

In astrology, no doubt the most ancient of organized esoteric studies, a person's "chart" is a schematic picture of the solar system at the time when that person was born. It shows where the Sun and Moon are in relation to each other, as well as the angles between all the planets at that moment as viewed from the birth place on earth.

I didn't see my own astrology chart until I was in my mid-fifties. Growing up in a Catholic culture precluded even considering such material okay to explore since "All forms of divination, the work of the devil, are to be rejected." American culture itself didn't give much consideration to in-depth astrology until the New Age movement called attention to this field of study, though it was/is still considered "fringe."

A good friend of mine had been introduced to astrology and knowing that I was open to new ideas, decided to buy me an astrological reading as a birthday gift one year. I wasn't terribly interested in astrology but decided to give it a chance and see what all the fuss was about.

At our session, the astrologer spread out several charts in front of me, each of which contained wheels and symbols and lines and all manner of scribbling about which I had not a clue.

However, when he explained what the symbols meant I was astonished. The chart showed both the Sun and Moon— those two most important "planets" in astrology—as well as several other planets as appearing in one particular section of the sky when I was born, indicating that I would likely have great interest in the topics associated with that area. In astrological terms, those themes are a major part of the life path for the soul born at that time and place.

That section of the sky, known as the Ninth House, has these themes: religion, long-distance travel, other cultures, philosophy, mental studies, collective mind, broader viewpoints, publishing, and law.

I was taken aback as the astrologer read these topics to me. I had already been actively engaged in almost all of them. I had intuitively been pursuing what astrology might call my "soul work." If I had been told about this life path in my teens, one could have said my activities were simply self-fulfilling prophecies. But that was not the case.

The astrologer explained that he viewed the chart and a person's life connected by "synchronicity" rather than cause and effect. That is, the clues in the chart "mirrored" what inclinations a particular soul had for this life, and the idea that it did so since birth was no issue if we let go of "time" as being strictly linear. Yes, rethinking "time" is a lot to digest.

Astrology put the paths I was already pursuing into the context of soul work, and that resonated deeply with me. I always sensed I was not simply a "tourist" in my travels, even though I certainly hit many tourist spots. The travel itself was an important experience, both the events that flowed easily and those that went awry, and astrology was a construct that helped me understand that and grasp the broader trajectory of my life. My chart was a confirmation of my choices in life.

Sure, if I were totally enlightened I wouldn't need confirmation, but alas...

My own words, "the travel itself was an important experience," echoed in my brain for days after I had written them. And those thoughts raised still another question for me: why do I often feel more "at home" when traveling than when ensconced on my living room sofa?

Where is Home?

WHEN I AM a stranger in a strange land, my hearing grows sharper, my eyesight keener. Temple bells reach me through traffic clamor, and the bright face of a raggedy youngster flashes out at me, inviting me to focus on his wide eyes and not his dirty hands or calloused bare feet. And my taste buds eagerly await the next unexpected flavors, even those I later choose not to experience again.

In that foreign land I *expect* I won't know how to act all the time, that some local practices will seem bizarre to me, that I will misunderstand and be misunderstood, that I might feel lonely and out of place. I expect that.

But I often feel lonely and out of place in my own country, I just didn't think it would be so.

In my case, I suspect that being a gay youngster set the scene for such feelings. Growing up in the 40s and 50s, every book I read, every radio program I listened to or TV show I watched all were peopled with straight folks—and their stories. "My" people were not there. I concluded I must be "the only one" and that "no one must ever know." Happily, times have changed, but the habit of feeling an alien, traveling through a "not my" culture—desperately trying to blend in—was already in place.

I am certain I was not alone in such feelings. Any youngster whose body was different—heavier, taller, shorter, other skin color than most, whatever—must have experienced the same thing. Or those for whom academics were not their forte, or whose creativity and looking at things differently was considered an aberration rather than a gift. As a friend once said, "Nobody gets out of childhood without a wound."

But my life has been overall a very blest one, and I do not dwell on those early challenges. I simply note to myself that when I feel "out of place" in a foreign culture, it's not a problem because "I know how to do that feeling." I've had years of practice.

Thus, I thrive on foreign soil, and, in perhaps a bit of a contradiction, sometimes feel more at home there than in my own birth land. I know well how to tread the path of "other" cultures, how to adapt, how to blend in to a certain degree. So, I travel. And when challenges loom large and almost overwhelming, I recall Chesterton's quip (paraphrased), "You can look upon this as an inconvenience or an adventure."

I choose adventure.

And I deeply resonate with this quote from W. Somerset Maugham in *The Moon and Sixpence* (and wish that such eloquence were my own).

> I have an idea that some men are born out of their due place. Accident has cast them amid certain surroundings, but they have always a nostalgia for a home they know not. They are strangers in their

birthplace, and the leafy lanes they have known from childhood or the populous streets in which they have played, remain but a place of passage.

They may spend their whole lives aliens among their kindred and remain aloof among the only scenes they have ever known. Perhaps it is this sense of strangeness that sends men far and wide in the search for something permanent, to which they may attach themselves. Perhaps some deep-rooted atavism urges the wanderer back to lands which his ancestors left in the dim beginnings of history.

Sometimes a man hits upon a place to which he mysteriously feels that he belongs. Here is the home he sought, and he will settle amid scenes that he has never seen before, among men he has never known, as though they were familiar to him from his birth. Here at last he finds rest.

In some ways I still search for that land. It may sound strange, but I have always had a challenge to simply "be here" physically in the U.S., especially after my few years in Asia.

Not long after I returned from my seven-year Asian sojourn, I attended a presentation by a panel of psychics, though I cannot remember what drew me to that event.

While interesting, most of the panelists seemed a bit woo-woo, even for me. The one that caught my attention was a slightly plump and jocular woman who gave her thoughts on being a psychic, then added, "Of course, what do I know, I'm just a Puerto Rican housewife." I liked her easy-going manner and appearing down to earth, so after the presentation I asked her if she saw individual clients. She did.

On the appointed day, she ushered me into her living room and handed me a basket of stones. "Take your time and pick one," she said. While my attention went to the stones, she was assessing me, she later told me.

"Hey, what's up with you? I've been reading your chakras and they're really strange. Your upper ones are spinning like crazy but your lower chakras are practically dead."

I knew enough about chakras—those vertically aligned energy-whorls in our body—to understand that the upper ones were concerned with expressing oneself, intuition, and spirituality, and the lower ones were about connection to the earth, sex, and personal power.

"You're like Brother Josephus who's been meditating in the Himalayas."

Jesus!! She knew only that my name was Jim. I had not told her I had just returned from Nepal and that I was—at that time—still a brother in a religious order. I figured I should listen to this woman.

"You need to ground yourself to this planet. Go up to Calistoga and get into those mud baths. Have a lot of sex. Get massage. And eat flavorful, spicy food."

I later danced out of her house, thrilled to have received a prescription for health that sounded oh so right for me.

And it all helped, somewhat. But often I still feel rather a stranger right here "at home"...

Choice, Accident, or Cosmic Plan?

I Never Planned It That Way

WHEN I THINK of the twists and turns—accidental meanderings—of my life's path, I have often wondered, "How did I get to *this* place which in fact has been a great catalyst for soul work?" I never expected that to happen, or planned it that way.

Almost all of us do our soul work "accidentally," in the sense that we are not necessarily conscious that that's what we're doing when we start it. That aspect of our inner work—its happening accidentally—may be clearer to us when hit by unusual events during travel, but it also happens at home.

Who among us has said something like, "I believe I'll go into real estate/medicine/teaching in order to do my inner work, my soul work"? Probably nobody. We are drawn to whatever profession for various reasons, most likely at an age when we are not thinking about "inner" work. We want to engage in work that attracts us, or make a good living, or perhaps please our parents as might be the case in taking over the family business.

As we learn our craft, however, we may begin to see the challenges in our work as vehicles for self-reflection and personal growth, not just outward obstacles to be overcome. When that happens, we are at the threshold of doing soul work and this can happen in any profession, any family situation, with any physical illness or disability that may come our way. And even if "fate" somehow lands us in a profession not originally of our choice, that vehicle can invite us into soul work as well.

I never expected to become a teacher.

Even though teaching has been, in different forms, my life's career—and joy. It is a craft I have developed, and has been an extremely satisfying profession. But I never chose it.

In high school we had a "career day" each year and representatives of various professions gave short talks about their work. We could choose which presentations we wanted to attend. And although we were surrounded by teachers on a daily basis, there was always a talk given by a teacher from another school. I never attended the "teacher" talks.

I chose journalism once. How exciting to be covering major disasters, or helping to solve crimes with my *astute* investigative reporting—I fantasized. Another time I listened to a talk by a member of the U.S. Navy. I had heard that at the end of basic training you took a round-the-world cruise. Now, *that* was cool. (Images of swabbing decks never entered my mind. I was a teenager.)

That all-boys high school I attended was taught by a religious order of brothers. These were caring, professional men of integrity. They were there for me when I needed them. They were generous people, and *above all* they impressed me as men who had *purpose* in life. I looked up to them and eventually decided I wanted to be like them. It only dawned on me later that I would therefore have to become a teacher because "That's what the brothers do." It was in fact a minor shock that I now had a profession cut out for me. No more waffling concerning which career path to follow.

But what to teach? I decided to teach what my favorite brothers taught—mathematics. While my decision may have had a strong element of hero worship, I have no doubt that deep intuition was at play there. I didn't know it then, but later came to see that not every important or wise choice came from syllogistic thinking. Sometimes the gut went right to the answer. Teaching mathematics was the right choice for me at the time, and after college I wholeheartedly threw myself into it.

Teaching a variety of students, with all their unique challenges, pushed me to deep levels of reflection and urged me to continually develop compassion. My students also—more often than I would have liked—provided the irritable grain of sand in the oyster shell which can produce something beautiful and valuable. What a gift for my soul the profession has been for me.

I certainly didn't consciously choose massage as a vehicle for soul work, but personal inner work was woven deeply into that endeavor. Nor did I, as a brother, volunteer for India to do soul work. At the time it seemed like an exciting adventure and a certain antidote for the blahs of my then-midlife crisis. Yet I accomplished some of my deepest soul work there.

Is there an obscure cosmic plan at work out there? Many of us would say yes.

Paradise Regained

Phuket Island, Thailand

FOR LUNCH I had fresh prawns in a red Thai curry sauce, for 100 Bhat, $2.50 USD. You can get almost anything on this lovely island resort for 100 Bhat. For slightly more than that I purchased a genuine look-alike Rolex watch. It's really quite chic. I've decided that when going through Customs I'll wear it. Those agents are generally focused more on searching luggage than people.

My hotel is a charming older hotel. It has only two stories— no claustrophobic elevator rides for me into a glitzy high rise— and surrounds a tropical garden and pool. Each room has high ceilings and French doors giving onto a private verandah. A delightful place.

Consistently listed by Conde Nast Traveler as one of the top ten island resorts in the world, Phuket has clearly bounced back after the devastating tsunami of less than a year and a half ago.

There are only a few telltale signs of that disaster: souvenir photographs of the waves crashing in and their aftermath, spanking brand new "Tsunami Evacuation Route" signs, and the sidewalk along the main drag in horrible disrepair. Though the shops and restaurants are in great condition, getting to them is a challenge for your ankles. I had penned in my mind a strong letter to the authorities about the sidewalks when reason took over. Presumably sidewalks must be the last in the repair plan, after all electrical, gas, and sewer lines below have been fixed. We've all seen American streets that required two months to repave, only to be torn up the following week for underground work.

There's one other hint about the tsunami that I didn't catch at first. Patong Beach, the main beach here and a two-minute walk from my hotel, is a dazzling crescent-shaped beach with an unusually wide swath of white sand running about two miles. I thought it rather striking that the many hundreds of umbrellas that line the area were all the same orchid color. Then I realized they were all in perfect condition, quite clearly new, and sponsored by the Siam Mercantile Bank.

Somewhere in the Indian Ocean or nearby dumps lie the tattered and twisted umbrellas of old.

* * *

On December 26, 2004, the sun shone and warm breezes blew in on the shores of Thailand's famed resort beaches like Phuket Island, Phi Phi Island, and Khao Lak on the mainland.

Even by 9:30 a.m. many visitors had already rolled out of bed and begun to throng the beaches. For any number of Westerners, the "winter holidays" or Christmas holidays were seen as the ideal time to journey to warm climes. Thai people and citizens of nearby countries also enjoyed the relaxing atmosphere of what many called "paradise."

A strange event occurred just before 10 a.m. The sea began to retreat from the shore and exposed large areas of sandy beaches not seen before. A curious phenomenon it was, and people exclaimed, "The tide is going out, and so fast!"

Eerie videos show people running out to explore the newly exposed beach—and unknowingly rushing to their death.

Earlier that morning around 8 a.m., the Indian tectonic plate had slipped under the Burma plate along a line of roughly 900 miles and caused the third largest earthquake ever recorded. Its duration, between eight and ten minutes, was the longest ever recorded. Its ultimate consequence, the death of at least a quarter million people in thirteen countries, could hardly have been foreseen.

The earthquake, its epicenter in Indonesia, had spawned not one but several reactionary waves that came to be called a tsunami and which took less than two hours to reach Thailand. As these waves crashed in on each other, they drew water out to themselves creating what is called "the disappearing sea effect" or "tsunami drawback." This seemingly benign event is a harbinger of death. It is usually less than five minutes after the drawback that the major waves begin to appear. And once a tsunami crashes on land and lays waste to lower areas, its retreat back to the ocean is equally devastating. Anyone caught in the immense force of water going either way is most likely doomed.

In Phuket, many of those who had survived the first wave—which meant none of those frolicking on the curious new beach—were lulled into a false security. As they returned to the beaches and hotels, a second wave struck and took its now predictable price.

The tsunami had an even more devastating effect at the seaside resort of Khao Lak on the mainland. Because of its low-lying terrain, with only bungalows and not cement high-rise hotels, waves ranging from 30 to 100 feet exacted a death toll much higher than at Phuket and Phi Phi.

On one beach, a young girl was taking a "tourist ride" atop an elephant. When the wave crashed there, the elephant's instinct to run farther inland saved the girl's life. Others on the beach were not so fortunate.

At still another beach resort, a young woman watched helplessly as her sister, clinging to a door frame standing alone without a wall, eventually succumbed to the raging waters and drowned. At a hotel in Phuket, a number of guests managed to climb fire escapes to reach the fourth floor where they viewed waters carrying debris and struggling people past them. Hands reached out to grab desperate souls, sometimes successfully but mainly in vain. And so the stories went.

Later, an odd secondary casualty of this disaster was the plight of Thai fishermen. Many were reduced to near poverty because Thai people were concerned that locally caught fish may have fed on human remains washed out to sea. Only when the Director General of WHO appeared on Thai television to announce that he ate fish from the area every day did the tide on that issue slowly turn.

* * *

Even after learning more about the tsunami, I still like my low-rise hotel. Such unthinkable disasters only happen to *other* people, right? But what other attitude is a viable one?

As you, Gentle Readers, know, I live in California and cannot spend my day wondering about the next earthquake. In just one year of living in Nebraska I experienced a summer of extreme drought, the worst in 50 years, and witnessed—from the safe position of the school rooftop—a tornado rampaging across our area of town. I was earlier stranded in a snow blizzard with 30 high school seniors for several days at a country retreat house. We were safe, electricity held, but it required four-wheel-drive vehicles to bring food in for us.

I want to be neither cavalier about possible real dangers, nor paranoid about crossing the street. And no use in confining oneself to one's own home in hopes of staying safe. We're told that most accidents occur there.

And so I find myself letting such tragic events as the tsunami fade into the past and, like many others, focus on the trivia of everyday living.

To wit—my hotel is happily devoid of my main complaint about hotel rooms worldwide: an air-conditioning unit that blows directly onto your bed. My room does have AC, but its fans are directed toward a wall from which the cool air ricochets nicely about the room.

I've managed to work around my other two complaints about the universal hotel room. First, they all have eternally plumped foam pillows ten inches high which are designed to dislocate all your cervical vertebrae. I suppose they *look* good on the hotel brochures. "Oh, such luxury!" I spoke to housekeeping while making appropriate grimaces and neck twistings to obtain a thinner pillow, which they finally produced.

It seems we have a planetary culture of the *visual*, one that lacks recognition of the kinesthetic experience. Did the room designers ever sleep on those pillows? We also seem to choose the visual over taste, gastronomic taste that is. I'm reminded of the strawberry shortcake photos on shiny plastic menus in the U.S. that showcase humongous strawberries covered in a glistening sugary syrup, which in reality are totally tasteless—except maybe for the high-glycemic glaze. What's the point?

Surely you're dying to know my other hotel issue: quilts on every bed, even in the tropics. Whatever are they teaching people in those pricey Hotel Management courses in Switzerland?

I pulled my quilt out of its casing and I use that container as a sheet which is enough covering. After several days the housekeeping ladies have acquiesced and no longer stuff the quilt back into its sleeve.

Oh dear, do I sound like a whiner? This place really is lovely and deserves better press. The hotel pool has a swim-up bar where the Mai Tai's flow and one need only splash over to the pool ladder to heft oneself out and crash onto a lounge chair for a quick snooze.

I arrived here with a slight throat infection which soon got less "slight" and I could barely speak. The other day I visited a walk-in clinic where the doctor prescribed penicillin for me, a four-day course. Does that sound right? I've never heard of taking antibiotics for only four days, so, as a somewhat hypochondriac Virgo, I marched into another pharmacy and purchased a couple more days' supply. I'm doing much better.

However, I had "lost my voice" for a while. (How curious, I have also not been writing the last few days...)

Evenings are spent exploring streets packed with semi-open-air restaurants and eyeing the large fish and seafood items sitting on counters lined with chipped ice. Restaurants all have roofs, presumably because of the sun and the monsoons, but most have at least two sides open to the elements—and tropical breezes blow in. The food is fresh, reasonably priced, and exquisitely tasty.

I haven't had much interaction with locals here. Perhaps that's because the place is so egregiously touristy that maybe Thais want to keep to themselves. But I am content. Phuket is warm, clean, and quiet—just what I came for after the tension in Nepal.

Where Are The Philippines?

Manila, Philippines

I MUST CONFESS, dear friends, that I thought the Philippines—named after King Philip II of Spain—were in the middle of the Pacific Ocean. Not so. The 7000+ islands in this archipelago lie basically below China in the South China Sea and the capital, Manila, is approximately 700 miles southeast of Hong Kong. The name Manila was derived from a type of plant grown in that area, the unbleached pulp from which was the material for the original "manila envelope."

Today the capital is a bustling town of some 15 million people, said to be the most densely populated city in the world (it seems I've read that about four different cities) where the current "cold weather" season averages 86–90 degrees Fahrenheit with 90 percent humidity. Remind me not to visit here in the "hot season."

I'm in the Philippines at the invitation of my old friend from India days, Brother Richard. He now lives in the southern Philippines where he administrates a project similar to the work with street children he did in India, and had come up to Manila to meet me and guide me around. He is a genuinely good and generous man.

Last night we strolled Baywalk, the oceanside promenade where the seawall runs a mile or so along outdoor cafes, restaurants, and bars, almost all of which sport a live band playing familiar American songs. Many Filipinos are highly talented musically and numerous bands are bundled off to play in Japan and in other Asian countries' nightclubs. Even on weekday nights, practically every café on Baywalk is packed, and on weekends the throngs in thongs—footwear—leave barely a square inch available to squeeze by.

If you are visiting the Philippines, please carry several bottles of Gatorade when you roam Manila. I sweat without pause and, concerned that I might faint from loss of salt and sugar, I found myself at McDonald's replenishing these nutrients with a hot fudge sundae. Here, I consider that a health food.

This is a very Catholic country, in fact the third largest "Catholic country" in the world, quite a surprise for an Asian state. On any Sunday you'll have three or four Masses being said in each of several local shopping malls. People gather on the balconies surrounding the mall atrium, look down and sing hymns, then between religious songs slip into their favorite store for bargain jewelry.

Manila has an elevated metro system, a mammoth benefit in a highly congested city. Filipinos appear generally quite polite as 80 of them mash into a coach built for 40. I have no trouble communicating with them because English, besides Filipino, is an official language and has been the medium of instruction in public schools since the early 1900s. However, on the streets and in the malls I almost never hear friends chatting in English. One's "mother tongue" is so called for obvious reasons and its hold on our psyche is practically ironclad.

A Skimpy History of Western Presence in the Philippines

HOW DID ENGLISH become the language of public school instruction in the Philippines?

Let's go back a bit. The first European documented to visit the Philippines was that renowned sailor/navigator we all read about in elementary school, Ferdinand Magellan. He was the one, you remember, who gave the Pacific Ocean its name and led the voyage for the first circumnavigation of the globe. A Portuguese explorer, he came to the attention of the king of Spain who commissioned him to find a westward route to the famed Spice Islands (the Maluku Islands in present day Indonesia).

Magellan set out with a crew of 270 and five ships, though only 18 of the original crew and one ship would complete the journey. Disease and war would take its toll. By the time Magellan reached the Philippines in March 1521, a year and a half after departure from Spain, he was already down to a crew of 150 and three ships.

Along the way, several ships had mutinied. Those ships were captained by Spaniards who were not happy serving under a "mere" Portuguese leader. Matters worsened when

Magellan announced that rations would be cut as they waited out the winter on the southeast coast of South America, where a few men had already died of cold. Magellan defeated that uprising, and a few mutineers were said to have been hung, drawn, and quartered. Sir Francis Drake found their bones years later.

Although Magellan spared the lives of some men he desperately needed for navigation purposes, karma would eventually come into play as he later faced his own gruesome death in the Philippines.

At that time the Philippines was not a single country but a patchwork of multiple "kingdoms" spread out over the several thousand islands. Magellan had been received well by a number of friendly "princes" on some the islands and even had success in converting a few of them to Christianity. One of these princes somehow convinced Magellan to attack his nearby enemy. It seems that part of Magellan's willingness to engage those neighbors was his hope of also converting them to the religion of European colonizers.

The natives in question launched a counterattack, and Magellan was at first only wounded in the arm. But seeing the man's vulnerability, the locals set upon him with bamboo spears and sharp cutlasses and made mincemeat of him as most of his crew fled back to their ship.

This initial foray into the Philippines gave Spain the right—at least so it seemed to Spain—to claim all the islands in the archipelago as their own, and they set about colonizing the area with Spanish families and institutions.

Fast forward to 1898, the Spanish-American War. The U.S. had been in favor of neighboring Cuba's independence from

Spain and when a mysterious explosion occurred on the USS Maine in the Havana harbor, killing 260 crew and causing it to sink, the U.S. declared war on Spain.

The war was fought both in Cuba and in the Pacific.

In Cuba. Remember Teddy Roosevelt and his Rough Riders charging up that hill? That effort in the Spanish-American War was successful though immense casualties were sustained by both sides, and San Juan Heights might be called the original Hamburger Hill.

Far away in Manila Bay, Philippines, Commodore George Dewey won a decisive war against the Spanish fleet, and Spain sued for peace. The resulting treaty gave the U.S. temporary authority over Cuba as well as "ownership" of Puerto Rico, Gaum, and the Philippine Islands—and gave Spain an identity crisis as a colonial power. The loss of Spain's last remaining colonies in the Pacific and the Americas was a profound shock to the Spanish national psyche and was the catalyst for an unprecedented philosophical and artistic reevaluation of their society.

Early on, American administrators in the Philippines established English as the medium of public education. As a result, the U.S. is the beneficiary of many immigrant Filipino nurses, teachers, and other skilled workers already proficient in English.

Though the U.S. needed to crush at least one revolution in the islands, it nevertheless set in motion a process for Philippine independence. That long route unfortunately was interrupted by two world wars, the second of which included Japan occupying the Philippines in 1942. Following the conclusion of that war, the Treaty of Manila in 1946 established an independent Philippine Republic.

In 1947 the U.S. was granted a 99-year lease on several military and naval bases although the Philippine government later rescinded that agreement. The last U.S. forces left the islands in November 1992.

Historically, the relationship between the two countries has been strong, with more than 90 percent of Filipinos consistently viewing the U.S. and Americans favorably.

Malady

IN PRESENT DAY Manila, I begin my morning with dried, salted fish and rice—who woulda thought it'd be so tasty? My body craves salt, I think that's it. But there is another reason that breakfast is appealing to me. It's the rice. I have learned to really like fried rice, and I can eat rice but not a lot of other breakfast staples.

1996

The itching at first was just annoying. It didn't occur every day, but when I scratched my abdomen, red welts would appear. Eventually the welts vanished but then my legs and arms began to itch. I thought that would also soon disappear, and it did, but returned shortly thereafter with even more intensity.

The constant discomfort completely upset my plans. After seven years teaching at the massage school, I had decided to leave and devote time to writing about my experiences in India and Nepal. I would keep my private massage clients to maintain an income. But now even seeing the occasional client was difficult, and focusing on writing was out of the question.

Everybody had a theory about the cause of the itching.

"It's the chlorine in the water supply. Let me sell you this shower head that will remove the chlorine." I bought the (costly) shower head but it didn't do the trick.

"I think the problem is all the toxins you've accumulated in your body. They are rising to the surface and exiting through the skin. You're going to feel great fairly soon now." Nope.

"The cause might never be known, and the itching will likely go away on its own. In the meantime, make a paste of oatmeal and slather it on your skin." I didn't really give that one a try—not that it would have helped my situation, I later learned.

My "new age" friends asked, "What are you 'itching' to do?" I impatiently dismissed that idea because the only thing I was "itching" to do was my writing, and now I was prevented from engaging in it.

My doctor referred me to an allergist, with the added suggestion that Dr. W. become my new primary care giver since I might need to see him quite frequently. Over the next several weeks I went for blood tests that Dr. W. ordered—and eagerly awaited the results. Meanwhile, even though he had put me on heavy doses of prednisone to gain symptomatic relief—and Xanax to calm down the agitation created by both the itching and the prednisone—my condition worsened.

I now spent the better part of an evening just scratching my legs. It was both pleasurable and painful. The Xanax helped me to sleep deeply, but that deep state masked my scratching my body unconsciously during the night. In the morning my sheets were bloody. My skin was becoming intolerably dry, and my hair was falling out in patches.

The series of allergy tests kept coming back negative and Dr. W. was getting impatient with me. One day he said, "The problem is that you're neurotic. You'd be better off seeing a psychotherapist than coming in here."

I was stunned. I can't even recall how I responded in that moment. Months later when I was healthy, I thought of all those cool things I "coulda/woulda/shoulda" said. "Okay, I'm neurotic. Now let's deal with this itching." "You're right, I really would get more out of a session with a counselor than seeing you. Way more." I later realized that the best professional response from him would have been to send me to another doctor for a second opinion, but he didn't.

Why didn't I myself insist on a second opinion? I was too exhausted to think clearly. I was still in great discomfort, scratching, bleeding, scarring, and on heavy medication. My mind couldn't focus. I returned home that day more discouraged and agitated than before—and took an extra Xanax.

A major lesson I learned from this health episode is the importance of having a health advocate when you are seriously ill. The sick person who is weakened physically, emotionally, and mentally from a serious chronic condition often can't handle their own advocacy. We need a guardian angel.

My guardian angel materialized in the form of a friend, Coralie. I had known Coralie and her husband, John, for several years already, through a mutual friend—the most common way I have increased my circle of friends. The three of us had spent many an evening talking about our lives, what's important to us, and sipping the over-sized martinis John made. (Coralie was much more abstemious in the martini matter than John or myself.)

I told Coralie, who was very interested in health care, that I was willing to try anything, *anything*, to address my condition and that I was no longer confident in the care provided by the system I paid my monthly premiums to.

Coralie first of all provided the emotional support I needed at the time. I might talk to her several times a week as a "check in" on how I was doing. The severity of my condition seemed to fluctuate now and I couldn't figure out why. She also had suggestions as to which body lotions could help my dry skin. They did. At the time if I was to be away from home for more than three hours, I would need to carry lotion with me and find a private place to apply it to my whole body.

At one point she heard of a psychic healer who had a good reputation, a man trained in the Philippines as a shaman. She took me to see him, but I had no clear health improvement from my session with him.

I reminded myself that this was a health "journey," and not to be surprised the path was more winding than straight. The major break came when Coralie referred me to a nutritionist, Jerry S., who had greatly helped a friend of hers.

Jerry was full of questions. *What is your regular diet?* The usual American one. (Hmm.) *What would be a favorite meal?* Pizza and beer. (Hmm!) *What is a snack you are really fond of?* Apple fritters. (Whoa!)

"Look," Jerry said. "I know you already had allergy tests, but I will order additional tests for you. I work in cahoots with Dr. A. and he will automatically okay them—they need an M.D.'s approval—and then let's see." (To this day, years later, I remember he had said "in cahoots with." Who said that anymore, even then?)

A couple of weeks later, Jerry called me. "Do you have any bread in the house?" Of course. "Throw that out immediately." He said my test results had come back and that I mustn't eat wheat or barley or rye anymore, starting right then. "That includes pizza and beer." Oh.

"But I don't have food allergies."

"You have a severe gluten intolerance. Your numbers are literally 'off the charts.' This is serious."

"Gluten? What's gluten?"

"Dr. A. will explain that to you. He's not a member of your health care system, so you'll need to pay out of pocket but he is very good and can help you. Here's his number, call to make an appointment immediately. And no wheat in the meantime. Wheat is in soy sauce so forget Chinese takeout." One of my favorites.

Sitting across his desk from me in a regular suit, Dr. A. was approachable and thorough. "Let me tell you first about your small intestine. It has about the same surface area as a tennis court."

That was possible because of the many finger-like projections from the sides of the intestinal walls, called villi. This immense surface area is what enabled the body to absorb nutrients. The stomach sent only a few nutrients into one's system—delivering those items was mainly the job of the small intestine.

"Gluten is a protein found in wheat, barley, and rye. Some think oats as well." Gluten set off a complex chemical reaction in people like me, resulting in those villi becoming flattened, and the small intestine no longer capable of absorbing nutrients into the body because of the decreased surface area.

"You cannot eat food containing gluten ever again in your life."

"Why me? What did I do?"

"You didn't do anything wrong. It's probably because of your Irish background," Dr. A. said. As wheat traveled westward from the Tigris-Euphrates Valley—one theory went—its chemical makeup evolved over time. Gradually it was "bred" to have more and more gluten so folks could create bread "twists" and even "braided" bread. Gluten was actually like "glue" that enabled such contortions of dough to take place and not fall apart. By the time wheat reached farthest west, Ireland, its gluten content was quite high and the human digestive tract was not made for that.

"But I'm only one-fourth Irish," I said.

"That doesn't matter. This disease, called celiac disease, is both congenital and capricious." Dr. A. explained that celiac disease may affect one member of a family but not others. And people of any ethnicity could have the condition, but it was often more severe with the Irish.

"You've always had this condition, not absorbing food properly. It's simply gotten worse now. Were you a bit thin as a child?" Yeah, Skinny Jimmy was one of my nicknames when I was young.

"And did you tend to be cold?" Yes. If I was swimming in a Wisconsin lake too long, I would get cold and start to shiver long before other kids, a condition my older sisters always reported to my mother. "Mom, Jimmy's got the chills!" She would then insist, against my desire, that I come out of the water.

"Your intestinal tract has suffered trauma from gluten and so your body is not getting proper nutrients. This is why your hair is falling out. It's also not absorbing fluids, which accounts for your skin being so dry." And the itching was an allergic-like reaction of my body to gluten, which it viewed as a "foreign" body. "You can have rice and corn, but not wheat."

I left Dr. A.'s office feeling somewhat overwhelmed but hopeful. His rigorous dietary plan, which he called PINGFY—Pain In the Neck but Good For You—eventually did the trick. It took more than six months but I finally emerged from what seemed a pit of despair into good health.

However, even after I needed less and less prednisone to calm down my body, my system still wanted Xanax. I had decreased the dosage from two tablets a day to one, then to one-half. But if I didn't take the one-half pill my hands would shake. I cut it down to one-fourth a day, then to one-eighth, and eventually none at all. I was finally off Xanax.

After my meeting with Dr. A., I returned to the allergist, Dr. W., and showed him the test results indicating I was celiac and how that was the cause of the itching. He murmured something like, "Well, a food intolerance isn't the same as a food allergy." I gave him the coldest stare I could muster and told him he couldn't treat me with such disrespect as he had. And I fired him.

I now understand that being a (diagnosed) celiac has health benefits. Given that gluten—according to most sources—creates inflammation in the body, I apparently have greatly reduced that condition, one which seems to be at the heart of most chronic conditions. My joints move with ease, my cholesterol numbers are hunky-dory for my age, and my energy levels are high. It's an added health benefit that I can no longer have battered, deep-fried foods and that I have to make an effort to find pastries and cakes that are okay for me. I certainly never would have chosen to be celiac, but I cannot deny it has had strong physical benefits for me.

And there is that other lifelong lesson which keeps appearing: I am not in control of as much of my life as I'd like to think. If there is a condition I cannot change, I would be wise to simply accept it. Or at least not focus on its perceived negative side. There is no benefit in that, only suffering.

How many times do I need to learn this lesson? I thought I had already "got" that teaching. I take comfort in the words of Maya Angelou on this soul matter. "Yes, you got it, but at a certain level. You need to keep getting it at deeper and deeper levels."

So be it.

Intramuros, The Immaculate Conception, and the Afterlife

THE INTRAMUROS AREA of Manila is the Old Walled City from the Spanish regime. A good 95% of it was destroyed in WWII by American bombs aimed at the Japanese who took to this place for their final stand in Manila. Only one major Intramuros building survived that war, previous wars, earthquakes, typhoons, and Protestants—the Catholic church of San Agustin, established 400 years ago by Augustinian monks.

San Agustin's miraculous qualities have taken on mythic proportions, but it was its status as a living museum of antique art and architecture that drew my interest. I spent a good part of one morning taking in the history and beauty of the 68 hand-carved monks' choir stalls imported from Spain, the silver and brass carriages used to carry holy statues in procession, the brocaded clerical vestments, and the sixteen stunning chandeliers from France. All this and more are worth your visit next time you're in Manila.

The Cathedral of the Immaculate Conception is not far away and is impressive though highly rebuilt.

If you attended Catholic grade school taught by nuns you can skip the next three paragraphs.

Catholic lore: The "Immaculate Conception" refers to Mary's, not Jesus's, being conceived in the womb free from Original Sin—which we all inherited from Adam and Eve you know. The Immaculate Conception is celebrated on December 8, and nine months later is the little-known and only slightly observed birthday of Mary on September 8. She was a Virgo.

Jesus's "immaculate conception" is called the Annunciation. The Angel Gabriel "announced" to Mary that she would, while remaining a virgin, miraculously conceive by the power of the Holy Spirit—apparently immediately if she agreed, which she did—and that event is celebrated on March 25. Yes, nine months later is baby Jesus's birthday, December 25.

Why do I mention this? Because so many people seem confused as to all the statues of Mary, rather than Jesus, in churches called the Immaculate Conception. There is a massive Shrine of the Immaculate Conception in Washington, D.C. and it is quite worth seeing. You might as well get your Catholic culture correct if you're going to visit these places. After all, if you visited temples in India you wouldn't want to confuse Krishna with Shiva, would you?

I spent time sitting in the back of the church at Immaculate Conception, a space much quieter than the popular St. Augustin's. The faint smell of incense from countless services, and smoke from now-extinguished candles reminded me of my own growing up as a Catholic in the 40s and 50s.

I was a scrubbed-faced altar boy at Blessed Sacrament church on Milwaukee's south side.

Besides "serving" at morning Mass and Friday evening novenas to the Sorrowful Mother (attended by the "sorrowful mothers" of the parish), it was a notable event when we acolytes were taught how to light incense for Benediction, that curious fifteen-minute adjunct to the Mass or a stand-alone service which focused on the Host that was, we were told, the Body and Blood of Jesus.

A key part of the service—after bowing low to the golden sunburst monstrance that housed the Host—was the offering of incense, a symbol of our prayers rising to heaven. I was taught how to carefully light a small circular piece of charcoal in the bottom of a gold cage called a thurible. This cage was suspended on three gold chains (for the Trinity?) and one of us, the thurifer, swung it back and forth to keep it lit.

At the proper time, another altar boy would heap incense grains from a gravy-boat-shaped container onto the top of the charcoal, and the thurifer would continue to swing the device while scented smoke poured forth.

I used to love it. "Smells and bells" was a phrase often used to describe Catholic ritual, and it was fairly accurate. The Church was a Master Ritualist. We engaged in services that took us beyond our little selves and helped us understand we were part of a greater entity. The many symbols involved in the rituals indicated that "There is more going on here than meets the eye."

No wonder all those memories came to mind. It is said that smell is the sense most closely associated with memory. When entering a church infused with those smells of ritual, I am taken back many decades to memories of my youth. I cannot help myself.

And those were fond memories—until I entered pubescence. At that point I was told that the sexual thoughts I had, triggered by my hormonally fuming body, would send me to eternal hell should I dwell on them for more than a nanosecond. It was a tricky dance I engaged in, making sure I had been to Saturday Confession in time to be pure enough to receive Holy Communion at Sunday Mass.

Guilt is exhausting. Especially guilt which is manufactured by an arbitrary set of beliefs. So I have left that all behind. I have no need of "belief" in theoretical doctrines anymore. But have I really jettisoned *all* beliefs? When I think about it, there is one "belief" I still hold to: that of an afterlife.

Can I never fully escape the indoctrinations of childhood? That is a discouraging thought even though I *want* to hold to that particular belief. It gives me comfort. It feels right.

Upon further examination, I see at least two factors involved in that belief. It might simply be a consequence of the basic instinct of self-preservation. There is no more primal impulse than that of survival. Countless stories attest to that phenomenon. A drowning person will clutch at that straw, and a survivor of suicide attempts will speak of last-minute regrets. We are hard wired to preserve ourselves.

If the instinct to survive is true at the physical level, why would it not be true in the psycho-spiritual realm?

My studies in dream work offer still another explanation. Over millennia, dreamers have reported what are now called "visitation dreams." Such a dream occurs when a recently deceased loved one appears in a dream, but not just any dream. A visitation dream is marked by an unusual quality of light surrounding the deceased, and perhaps the imparting of information that only that person would know. Over time, the occurrence of such dreams likely engendered in the human race the "belief" in an afterlife. The dead still live on in some form, and are able occasionally to communicate with us, especially right after their demise.

From the point of view of dream work, the belief in an afterlife is not tied to any religion nor to any particular image of the afterlife. I have no belief in what the afterlife might look like. Is it in the context of heaven and hell? In the paradigm of reincarnation? Valhalla? Such specifics indicate a continuing belief in a particular religious background. No need for that.

I must also add that we use the word "belief" and "believe" in multiple ways, and that can cause confusion. We might say "I believe Jesus is the Son of God," or "I believe in the basic goodness of humanity," or "I believe I'll have another doughnut." The first example is one of a religious belief, the second of a "conviction," and the third of a desire. What a linguistic mess.

As I stepped out of my pew in the Cathedral of the Immaculate Conception, I genuflected toward the altar. Old habit, perhaps. Or maybe one of the many gestures we have at our disposal to acknowledge that, once again, "There is more here than meets the eye."

On another note, you've noticed that almost all Filipinos have Spanish surnames. It's not that the Spaniards married everyone in sight, but one day about 150 years ago, the Spanish Governor harrumphed, "These people don't have last names. That won't do. How can we organize them? Hand out family names to everyone. Ours will do nicely."

Last night Rich and I threw ourselves into an activity which is quite popular in Manila—malling. The upscale shopping and night life spot in Manila is called Makate, and the Ayala complex boasts some five or so shopping centers all connected by bridges, outdoor promenades on all three levels, garden centers, orchid pathways, and tunnels. And these are not your architecturally boring rectangular two-level strings of Penny's and Baskin-Robbins et al., but gracefully curved buildings with glass facades and atriums filled with top-notch performers.

After browsing book shops and gardens, we enjoyed tapas and drinks at three different trendy bars—along with five million Filipinos.

Last Stop

Davao City, Mindanao
Southern Philippines

LATITUDE, TWO DEGREES above the equator.

Attitude, beaucoup degrees above most cities, at least concerning smoking.

NO smoking in public, including city streets. Rich says the mayor is *quite* strong-fisted, so fear may be a high motivator for compliance.

This is the city where Rich has a skills training center for young boys and girls, and I visited there midmorning one day. The teenaged boy who shoveled fresh bread out of the large outdoor oven looked confident and proud of his work. And rightly so. Richard beamed. One thing I learned from my years in the Brotherhood is that helping others, especially disadvantaged youth, is a reward in itself.

The day had started early. Rich had roused me at 6 a.m. and took me to the morning fish market. At the half-acre covered market I saw five-foot long tuna, giant marlin, and a host of other fish I couldn't name.

We had a meal tonight of grilled, buttered shrimp caught *this morning*. I never knew how tasty truly fresh seafood is. No need for that spicy "cocktail sauce" that we use to kick up wooden prawns.

Nevertheless, I wouldn't trade my life of cool but sunny weather in Northern California for living an inch above the equator here. No, I love where I live even while traipsing here and there in territories new for me. And California now beckons...

When I pause to think what I have gleaned from this excursion apart from anything already mentioned, an event I have only briefly referred to surely makes the list. Attending the 25th Anniversary of the Brotherhood in India has reminded me again of how much my nearly 30 years as a brother shaped my life.

That life was an anchor for me, a solid footing from which to pursue higher education and a professional career of teaching. The support of my fellow-brothers in all my projects, especially the work in India and Nepal, was not just a comforting action—it was essential to the work and my own equilibrium. In addition, those years served as a catapult into the following, also satisfying versions of my life on this planet. Gratitude is my only response.

And visiting countries where tragedies I have known about have taken place—the tsunami in Thailand and the confinement of American citizens during WWII in the Philippines—makes those events more real, and engenders in me further compassion for our world family.

In fact, I have long held that the two most important virtues for me are courage and compassion. Courage to take a stand and make a contribution to humanity, and compassion to enliven individual acts with that which really counts. It is a goal toward which I continually strive.

Postscript

California, U.S.A.
2021

Rest In Peace

BROTHER RICHARD WAS murdered in full daylight on a street in Port-au-Prince, Haiti, in April 2013.

He had just withdrawn money from a bank and was crossing a street when a motorcycle carrying two men approached from behind. One grabbed the bag Richard was carrying and the other shot him three times in the back.

The incident was made to look like a robbery, but the real story is darker.

Some years earlier, the brothers had started works for the poor in Haiti, and local men had begun to join the religious order. In 2012, a gunman entered the brothers' training center and shot a young Haitian brother—just the one person, though other brothers were in the same room at the time. The gunman stole a computer, again apparently to make it seem a robbery. Eventually information came out that made a strong case for the murder being a gang rivalry killing.

The family of the murdered brother was supposedly part of a gang at odds with another gang. Was the murder a retribution for something? Most remaining Haitian brothers quickly scattered, though some wanted to continue their training. The local bishop, however, asked the brothers to close down their works for safety reasons. Richard, a French-speaking Canadian, had traveled to Haiti to assist any of the remaining brothers with obtaining visas for other countries where the brothers had institutions. All indications have pointed to Richard's murder being connected to the same gang situation.

None of the information above concerning rival gangs and possible motivation for the murders has been officially confirmed.

Upon hearing the news, I grieved his death. I had deep affection for this man, and even had a dream shortly thereafter about someone trying to call me on the phone, someone named "Richard." A contact from beyond? Who knows...

The Mayor
The mayor of Davao City in 2006 was Rodrigo Duterte, now the strongman President of the Philippines who is known for his extrajudicial killings of suspected drug dealers and other criminals. Duterte is also creating foreign policy to favor China more than the U.S., the country's historical ally.

The current mayor of Davao City is Sara Duterte-Carpio, daughter of the Philippine President. The vice-mayor is Sebastian Duterte, son of the President.

End of the Nepalese Monarchy
In June 2006, just months after my Nepal visit described here, the Nepal parliament took away the major powers of the king, reducing him to a figurehead. Two years later in 2008, as part of a peace deal with Maoist rebels, the

Constituent Assembly voted to abolish the monarchy—and the country became a republic. King Gyanendra and his family were given fifteen days to vacate Narayanhiti Palace in Kathmandu.

Gyanendra Shah now lives as a private citizen at Nagarjuna Palace, a complex of ten buildings given him by the government. He has recently stated he is ready to assume leadership in the country again should the people decide accordingly.

So, what does it mean to be a member of "royalty"? Here is my conclusion, and no offense to current members of royalty in any country: if you are a "royal," it almost always means that some place back in time, your ancestors were the warlords that won. That's all it means.

Bangalore
In 2014, the city of Bangalore was officially renamed Bengaluru.

2011

Delhi, Nepal, Cambodia, Myanmar

Getting There is Half the Fun –
In Business Class

San Francisco Airport Lounge
October 2011

IT'S BEEN TWENTY-FIVE years since I've been in Business Class and a lot has changed. So I might sound like a little kid grinning over his newly found treat.

I'm sitting in the British Airways Business and First Class lounge which Cathay Pacific uses in SFO, waiting for my flight to Hong Kong. Free internet, drinks, snacks, and wine and booze. By the time I finish this email it will be after 12 noon, so I might need to have a glass or three of wine.

After my last long trip I thought I was finished with international travel, then one day I glanced at my airline mileage plan and discovered I could fly anywhere in the world in Business Class. With free transportation and reasonable hotel rates in Asia—not to mention tasty, low-cost food, I can't afford to stay home.

We'll be boarding the plane directly from this comfy and quiet lounge, so I won't have to go through the noisy general lounge with all the "little people." Also, both check-in and security have special lines for special people like me. What a breeze—how will I ever fly coach again?

So far there are about fifteen of us in the lounge and it is deathly quiet. At the moment, I'm the only Anglo. The others look like well-heeled "Hong Kong Chinese." The women have stylish clothes, earrings ranging from tasteful to ostentatious, and strappy oh-so-trendy shoes. The men are slightly round-bellied businessmen types, no doubt engaged in hostile takeovers on their phones or laptops.

The finger food on the nearby buffet is all Chinese, naturally, but surely loaded with gluten-laced soy sauce, so I confine myself to packaged snacks. My choice is popcorn which I try to eat in an elegant manner. Elegant? Okay, tell me, how does one eat popcorn without looking like a preteen at a vampire movie? Taking a single kernel at a time makes no sense, so most of us pour a bunch into our cupped palm then push the whole deal toward our mouths—moving our palm around until we've forced everything inside—and then lick our salty hand. If you have another method, I'm waiting to hear it.

Oh, now some cowboy arrived and spilled his Pepperidge Farm Golden Butter Cookies on the floor as he ripped into the package. While he cleans up, I herd small popcorn bits from my couch into a napkin destined for the nearest wastebasket.

Miss Hong Kong of 1991 or so sits across the lounge with her Fendi bag and duty-free prizes, and has perfectly peeled an orange. It sits there, whole, like a golden globe with sinewy white meridians. I want to see how she attacks it for sustenance, but they've just called for boarding.

San Francisco to Hong Kong

MY BUSINESS CLASS cubicle is not terribly wide, but it is nevertheless private. There is a low wall between each section so you are not physically in contact with others. No need to arm wrestle for the arm rest.

The seat is recliner style, with ten control buttons, and will flatten out for sleeping. I've also brought along Ambien in case I'm restless, and sufficient ear plugs to supply the whole cabin.

While waiting for takeoff, I ambled forward to First Class to see what the scoop is there. Well! *Those* people each have an area they call a "suite"—enough walled space for you and a traveling troop of well-wishers.

There is even a "second" seat in your mini living room in the air should you be traveling with someone and wish to dine together. All this was explained to me by Miss Po Lan, a very sweet flight attendant from Malaysia according to her name badge.

"If you get bored Mister James, you come up here and try this place." Since there are nine such suites but only four were utilized on this trip, I did take her up on that offer toward the end of the flight and made the Hong Kong landing in super style.

Don't get me wrong, I am beaucoup happy in my little Business Class cubby. And the earphones are both cushy and astounding in terms of sound quality. Before dinner I luxuriated in the bright tones of Vivaldi, the quintessential classicism of Haydn, and the haunting Nocturnes of Chopin.

I can hardly remember the last time I spent more than five minutes listening to music *for its own sake*. So often music has been a "background" to something else I'm doing—reading, cleaning, driving, etc. I have to admit that, with streaming movies so available, I'd probably feel I really wasn't *doing* anything if I spent the entire evening in my favorite chair, staring vaguely into space and simply listening to music. Sure, going out to a concert is *doing* something, but what about music at home?

Earlier on, the captain announced that our flight plan will take us over Anchorage, Alaska, and Siberia before heading down to the South China Sea. He said it was to avoid certain winds, and I imagine it also has to do with flying the "great circle" route on our planet.

Whereas in plane geometry the shortest distance between two points is a straight line, in spherical geometry—former math teacher here—it's along a great circle, which is a circle, like the equator, whose center would also be the center of the planet. A slice off the top of the world along a specific latitude would not result in a great circle. An "A" to all who followed that.

Time, I think, for a nap before Hong Kong...

Travelers' Tip: When out and about, always take these five items, listed in order of importance:

Passport and necessary visas
Ticket and boarding pass

Money, which can usually get you anything else you might need

Emergency meds (I include Valium in this category.)

Ear plugs (In the 80s a wonderful film was made about India titled *Heat and Dust*. I thought it should be called *Heat and Dust and Noise*.)

Shopping for Happiness

MODERN HONG KONG airport is built on an island created just for that purpose. The old airport, Kai Tak, was nestled between water and skyscrapers and hills in Kowloon, the mainland part of Hong Kong. This tricky location earned it a high rating on the TV program titled World's Most Extreme Airports.

To reach Kai Tak your plane would skim the tops of highrise apartment buildings, make a dizzying sharp right turn, and aim for the runway. Because of the accompanying noise in residential areas, flights were banned into Hong Kong after 11 p.m. until the new airport was built. The old runway protruded into Victoria Harbor, and more than one aircraft skidded off into the drink. I didn't know this when I was there in the 80s, so to me it was just another landing—ho hum.

The new airport is a hundred times safer but unfortunately greets you with those standard gray corridors and vague signs. (What exactly is "disembarkation"?) But stick with it a bit, for when you shunt through the bottom level (Immigration and Customs) and arrive in the International Transit area, you step off the escalator into a land of lights and glitz and bling.

A soaring curved ceiling covers what may be the airport's main attraction: acres of sparkling duty-free shops which are strategically placed between you and your departure gate. You name it, they got it—if it's pricey. But I guess you feel you're getting a deal since you don't pay those duty taxes.

All that glitters is not gold, much of it is amber. In the liquor section I noted in particular the $5000.00 bottle of Remy Martin. The bottle's shape is indeed quite cool but I decided to pass it up, although I tried to take a picture of it and its price tag. A saleslady was immediately at my elbow admonishing me I couldn't do such a thing. "Security reasons," she said. Huh?

If all roads lead to Rome, then all concourses lead to the duty-free shops and back again should your attention falter. Where is my gate? Oh, there's that bottle of Remy Martin again.

When built in 1998, this behemoth airport was the largest passenger terminal in the world. I don't know if it still has that honor but I am duly impressed with this place. And the Business Class lounge is much larger and more bustling here than in SFO. No surprise since Hong Kong is home for Cathay Pacific Airlines and also seems to be the crossroads of Asia. I am here to pick up another flight onward to Delhi.

Of the 47 computer stations in the lounge only three are utilized—by myself and two other Luddites who aren't carrying a cell phone, tablet, or a laptop. Remember, this place was built right before the wireless revolution and folks now prefer to sit in comfy chairs with their electronic devices—closer to the wine and finger food—to shoot off into cyberspace.

Oh, the call has just come to shoot off into real space.

What's in a Name?

"EXCUSE ME SIR, are you Japanese?" said a flight attendant whose name badge announced she was Miss Puja.

"No, my name is Irish," I replied.

"Oh, I didn't think you were Japanese. But on my list your name is spelled the Japanese way, O-h-a-r-a. For Irish, it has the apostrophe, yes?"

I congratulated her on her distinctions, and she beamed.

I have always liked my last name but the digital world doesn't. Cathay Pacific's reservations website would not accept the apostrophe in my name. I was gently scolded by a red flag several times until I gave up and went Japanese. Then I fretted, needlessly it turned out, over those subsequent warnings that the name on my ticket "must be *exactly* as on your passport." Well, my name on my passport includes the apostrophe.

What's an Irish guy to do?

In stores and on the phone I have often heard, "Sorry, we don't have you in our computer." I coach them to try all the variations—with apostrophe, without, with capital H, with lower case h. "Oh, there you are."

Some digital input systems take the apostrophe and translate it to a "space." In several cyber places I have an alias: James O Hara. Junk mail periodically arrives addressed to Mr. Hara.

Miss Puja and I continued to chat, and based on an educated guess—her name, features, accent—I said something to her in basic Hindi. She was delighted and surprised. I gave her a bit of my background, and we were off comparing notes about Delhi. She had in fact been born and raised in Delhi and her in-laws had lived in the Civil Lines area of Old Delhi where I had also lived in the early 80s. We knew the same landmarks, the Oberoi Maidens Hotel, the Red Fort, the Jama Masjid, and more.

Another six degrees of separation thing.

Now, I need more food from the gourmet galley which we in Business Class can ask for at any time you know.

What day is it? Where am I? Am I Japanese?

Midnight in Delhi – Quite Unlike "Midnight in Paris"

New Delhi, India

WITH FEW EXCEPTIONS, most long-haul international flights arrive or depart New Delhi's Indira Gandhi Airport between midnight and 3 a.m. It has always been thus. One explanation I heard was that it would be a challenge for larger aircraft to land or, especially, to take off in Delhi in 115–120 degrees daytime temperature.

Aware that making good travel decisions through bleary eyes and a jet-lagged mind in the wee hours is iffy, I had made arrangements online for my favorite hotel—great location, happy rates. I walked briskly and with confidence through Immigration and the Green (Nothing to Declare) Channel.

Outside I hurried past the hordes of independent taxi drivers calling to me and chose one from the queue of "airport certified" vehicles. "Certified" means that the airport keeps track of them and you. Your name, destination and the taxi number are recorded in a tattered little book in the unlikely event something untoward should happen.

The grim ride at 2 a.m. into the city is certainly improved over yesteryear. Before suburbs edged up to the runways, the road between the airport and city center was long, deserted, and potentially dangerous. Your taxi might get stopped by thieves who relieved you of extra baggage.

Once, years ago in Delhi, a friend of mine was taking me to the airport at 5 a.m. on his motorcycle. Before we left he removed his wrist watch and explained why. Just the month before, his arm jewelry had been noticed by local thugs on that road and not so politely—he still had a facial bruise—confiscated, along with all his cash. Our trip that morning had gone smoothly.

Now, closer in to Delhi, as my taxi inched down garbage-strewn alleys and around packs of dogs, I knew something was amiss. Even the driver fidgeted, tapped his fingers on the steering wheel, and appeared hesitant to alight from the vehicle to ask directions from the raggedy denizens of Delhi noir still roaming about.

Cutting to the chase. "My" hotel had changed its name and another hotel in this seedy part of town had latched onto that old name. One more glance out the taxi window at the hotel entrance wedged in between a snack shop and an electrical supplies store helped precipitate a quick decision.

"Let's get outa here," is what I wanted to say—the most often used line in American movies I'm told—but I wasn't sure my taxi wallah would appreciate it fully. A fairly literal translation of what I said in Hindi is, "This is a bad place. We will go."

Now, I don't pretend to know a lot of Hindi anymore and the driver understood basic English, but certain survival phrases are etched in my brain and pop out easily. I'll bet several of you travelers out there can say "Where is the bathroom?" in multiple languages.

Deepak—name badges are so helpful—headed toward Connaught Place in the city center and eventually pulled up in front of the Hotel Asian International. "This is a good hotel for you." It turned out he was right. I'm glad I gave him a healthy tip.

To bed, to bed, I'm practically dead...

The 1911 Restaurant and Bar

"IN 1911 KING Emperor George V and Queen Empress Mary declared New Delhi the capital of India." So stated the first page of the menu at a nearby luxury hotel. Previously the capital had been Calcutta.

This amazing turn-of-the-century hotel (19th c. – 20th c.), aptly named The Imperial, is a gem of architecture and art and a repository of history. White pillars guard all entrances, high ceilings grace the lobby, and gilded interiors are the real deal not Las Vegas veneer.

I spent the last half hour examining old lithographs, photos, and drawings that line the hallways and adorn the side rooms. It's a history lesson on the Raj, British rule in India. I understand that some might not find such crass imperialism very charming, but it is history and that Empire did give the world its most international language today. Sure, study Mandarin, good idea, but 10,000 characters just to get started? Okay, I'm lazy.

Why am I in Delhi? From a practical point of view, it's where my freebie flight could take me and allow me to recover from jet lag before visiting friends in Nepal. Also, I have a certain nostalgia for Delhi where I lived in the early 80s, although the film *Midnight in Paris* was an insightful and entertaining reminder about the pitfalls of romanticized nostalgia. I shall try to avoid that.

In the restaurant, the "Curried Prawns, Goa style" just arrived and is absolutely the best I've ever tasted. Goa is a former Portuguese colony on India's west coast, south of Bombay/Mumbai, which I had visited many times in the 80s.

Before my time on the Subcontinent, in the 60s and early 70s, Goa with its wide beaches and swaying palm trees was the winter hangout for foreign potheads who then drifted up to cooler Kathmandu for the summer. In those days marijuana and its cousin drugs were legal in Nepal so the hippies had a grand old time on Freak Street at shops like the famous Eden Hashish Centre. The menu included items such as Hashish Toasted Cheese Sandwich and Hashish Cake, to be washed down with Hashish Lemon Tea or Hashish Milk Coffee. Colorful posters for this establishment headlined Hindu gods and today are collectors' items.

The Nixon administration, waging its "war on drugs," put pressure on the Nepali government to outlaw marijuana, so the giddy legal party came to an end in 1973.

For Goa, a major draw besides the beaches, was its exotic food—Indian yet touched with a Portuguese European flavor. And that remains true and legal today.

I'm back in India and enjoying its fabled curries while a live band in the adjacent bar plays the "Love Theme from The Godfather."

The Delhi Metro

WHEN THE FIRST line of this system opened on Christmas Day in 2002, 1.2 million people showed up for a joy ride. That line's capacity was 200,000. Extra police were called out for crowd control, and radio and TV announcers implored folks to stay home.

I don't know if there is another city metro built completely new since 2002, but this seven-line system is modern, high tech, comfortable, and clean. If only the crowds would stay home.

I have never been on any transit system in the world where the public address announcements were so clear. Crystalline is an understatement. Given first in Hindi and then in English, the announcements are simultaneously displayed in both languages (in their respective different alphabets) at the ends of each coach. System grids are also displayed throughout, with a green light indicating the current position of the train.

In the stations helpful signs encourage good behavior. "Take the stairs, stay healthy." (Don't crowd those escalators.) "No spitting." (In Hindi, Punjabi, and English.) "Spitting is not allowed." (Repetition helps.)

Famous for punctuality, the system boasts a rate of only one train in a thousand late since 2002. "Late" is defined as not within sixty seconds of the schedule, supposedly the strictest standard in the world.

The sleek coaches, built in Germany and South Korea, slide along almost silently. And there is no potentially dangerous "electric 3rd rail" as in the San Francisco Bay Area and Washington, D.C. systems. Electric power comes from an overhead source connected to the coach with an antenna-like conductor, as with Indian railways.

Security is high level. Like all hotels 2-stars or more, Metro passengers are scanned and given a pat-down and packages are x-rayed. You may recall the recent terrorist attacks on hotels here. They are taking no chances with the Metro in the nation's capital.

My first trip was a shock. People offered their seats to me and to others with packages. No pushing, shoving, or rude behavior. Orderly queues and smiling ticket sellers were the order of the day.

My second excursion was different. Transit police stood at every coach door to hold back departing passengers so the others could actually exit. Those same cops later pushed the newcomers more tightly into the coach so the doors could close. I waited for the next coach, slightly better. Rush hour dynamics are cross-cultural.

One day, I took the Metro out to my old neighborhood. After exiting at the proper station and a short walk, I escaped the frenzied main street, turned down a shaded lane, and entered the oasis—take that rather loosely—of the Civil Lines area where I had lived.

The Raj's government staff lived in this area and built stately homes with wide verandahs, balconies, and luxuriant gardens. Those houses still remaining are water-stained and crumbling but many of the trees survived intact. The shade and sounds of birds chirping are what hit you first as you turn off the main road and head down Sri Ram Marg.

Many owners of the once-grand homes have sold their valuable property, for a hefty sum no doubt, to folks building condos or apartment buildings. Sound familiar? My old place was/is a three-story apartment building which had connecting staircases inside and enabled the eight of us, four Americans and four Indians, to live fairly comfortably as if in one large residence.

Now, air conditioners jut from windows of the rooms where we used to swelter and the then-teenage son of the landowner, who lived next door, has his lawyer's shingle out front. The street is still the narrow lane it always was which may have saved it from being overrun by retail stores, and I have no doubt that neighbors still know everybody else's business. Back then friends looking for us were often greeted by the cigarette seller, who perched cross-legged and serene—or bored—in a niche of our building's wall.

"The Americans have all gone out. You please come back in one hour, that is their usual time."

It was pleasant to see the old place, but it's almost like looking at an old photo album. I'm not there anymore. I've left it all far, far behind.

My last Metro foray was to visit the tomb of Humayun, the second Moghul Emperor. Poor Humayun, he was seen as an able administrator but he made a fatal misstep, literally. While permitting the public to view his personage—*darshan*—one winter afternoon, he heard the call of the muezzin to prayer. In his fervor he dashed down slippery steps, fell, hit his head, and thus passed on the imperial crown to his son Jahangir.

In appreciation—I mean respect—Jahangir built the great tomb complex which was the precursor of the Taj Mahal. The grounds contain not only that tomb but many other sepulchers, gardens, channels for rose water that cooled the area in times past, and trees everywhere.

As I awaited my return train, I thought of my two disappointments in Delhi, a city I still have great affection for.

First, Delhi has become even less pedestrian friendly than before. Whereas some Western cities have banned cars in certain areas to promote strolling, casual shopping, and eating al fresco, I don't think this concept has yet touched the Indian psyche. Crossing a street now may require going several blocks out of your way because of median barriers and humongous roundabouts where even intrepid pariah dogs will not venture.

Second, the weather in October is still in the mid-90's and humid. I should have taken Al Gore more seriously and booked a November trip. October used to signal cool, green, and crisp. Sure, increased population is a factor, but I'm told the prolonged heat of the monsoon season is true in many rural areas at this western edge of the Gangetic Plain.

Back to the Metro. Kudos to the planners and builders of an amazing and much needed system.

And farewell to Delhi.

Errata

IN AN EARLIER email I had said that Humayun's tomb was built by his son Jahangir. Oops. It was built by his son Akbar. And Akbar's son was Jahangir.

I get the Mughal emperors confused because they were all impatiently waiting for dad to croak, or they helped the process along or imprisoned him, or similar. After one of those sons attempted to overthrow papa, the beleaguered emperor had the guy blinded. He couldn't bear to kill his son but had to render him useless.

This drama has played out repeatedly on the world stage of history. You can think of many examples yourself, various dynasties in different countries.

The Greeks had a story for this as they did for everything. Cronus was getting tired of his bossy and domineering father Uranus, so once when he was really, really irritated he castrated and killed the old grouch. Cronus knew that he could suffer the same fate himself from his sons, so he swallowed his children as soon as they were born.

His wife, however, hid one of the kids—Zeus—in a cave and guess what? That's right, Zeus eventually offed his old man.

Myths have powerful, symbolic lessons for us mortals. At a *metaphorical* level, all sons must castrate and kill their fathers in order to fully own and embrace their own masculinity and rightful place in the world. This is internal work, mind you.

If you think the above is a harsh metaphor, recall the revered Zen saying, "If you meet the Buddha on the road, kill him." Again, to be done inwardly, not outwardly. The light of wisdom must eventually shine from within each individual, and not be limited to and dependent upon buddhas, gurus, priests, popes, rabbis, ayatollahs, or whomever.

Beyond Religion

WHEN IN MY own life I had "killed the buddhas" of childhood conditioning, I found myself "beyond religion." Some may think that an arrogant or delusional attitude, but it is simply where I am at this point on my life's journey.

"Beyond" is not necessarily "better," unless that is one's true current path. I could have taken out my irritation with the Church's insistence on following its precepts blindly in my 20s or 30s by harrumphing and saying I was beyond religion. But I doubt that attitude would have had the same depth and authenticity as when I came to that point in my 40s.

By my mid-forties, and living surrounded by a diversity of religions on the Indian Subcontinent, I concluded that the theological assumptions of all religions were equally arbitrary and most of us had unwittingly flown into that sticky web.

During those India years, a gentle lesson came my way about the danger of being so immersed in one religious tradition that no other value system can be "seen."

The Thing to Do

1980

A half-day's bus ride northeast of Delhi lay the Lower Himalayas and the resort town of Mussoorie. At 6500 feet, Mussoorie was a cool oasis during May and June—which Indians called the Hot Weather—and happily possessed a language school. Learning Hindi, the most common language of northern India, combined with escape from the hot plains, sounded perfect.

I found myself there one summer, attending classes at Landour Language School and staying at a nearby guesthouse.

On the paths that crisscrossed the side of the mountain, I was surprised to encounter a number of Americans, mostly Protestant ministers, who were "old hands" in India. One of them, Mrs. Smith, wife of a thin-faced minister, liked to gather other foreign Christians around her table for luncheons of chicken salad, peas, and boiled potatoes.

During my second week in the mountains, I accepted an invitation from Mrs. Smith for "Saturday next at noon, then." At the dining table, covered with a yellowing linen cloth, I sat next to a young American, David, and his Vietnamese wife, Mei Ling. David, an energetic man supported by his church in America, had recently come to India to work with leprosy patients. I was about to ask him for details when Mrs. Smith, returning from giving directives to the cook, took her place and asked us to hold hands while she closed her eyes and prayed.

Mrs. Smith was not unpleasant looking, though she had a rather large nose which, because of her matronly figure,

I had hardly noticed. Until, however—after praying devoutly—she leaned forward to direct the table conversation.

"It's so good to have you here," she said to me. "We need young blood to continue making Christian inroads in this country."

"Actually, my focus is more..."

"India can be difficult, but be courageous when spreading the gospel. This country is in great need, these people are in such a wretched state." Turning to Mei Ling, she added, "Don't you agree, my dear?"

Mei Ling spoke softly. "Yes, our cook's wife is very sick and needs medical attention, but he has hardly any money."

"Well..., yes, a terrible physical state too," Mrs. Smith said, and called over her shoulder for the bearer to bring more water. "If he doesn't appear at work on time, I can find you another cook."

"Oh, I like this cook. But he was so stressed I gave him extra pay and a day off to take his wife to the hospital."

"Why, Mei Ling, how good of you," Mrs. Smith said, her fork poised over a small potato. "What a Christian thing to do."

"I'm Buddhist," Mei Ling said.

Soul Hypnosis

"BLESSED ARE THEY who have not seen and yet have believed." John 20:29.

I consider these to be highly dangerous words.

"Doubting Thomas" elicits this comment from Jesus in the scene in the Upper Room.

At that point, Jesus had been crucified, buried, and said to have risen from the dead. But during his first appearance to the disciples, Thomas was not present. When told "The Lord has risen," Thomas replies he would not believe it unless he could put his finger in the nail wounds in Jesus's hands and place his hand in his opened side.

A week later, Jesus again comes to the disciples, including Thomas this time. Jesus invites Thomas to place his fingers and hand into his wounds, to which Thomas replies, "My Lord and my God!"

"Because you have seen, you have believed. Blessed are they who have not seen and yet have believed."

This story appears only in the Gospel of John, none of the others. That Gospel's classic opening lines, "In the beginning was the Word, and the Word was with God, and the Word was God," indicates how heavily bent on "theology" and ensuring that the reader sees Jesus as "one" with the Almighty the following narrative will be.

The implication of those opening words and those later addressed to Thomas is that since Jesus is part of the Godhead, it would behoove us to trust everything he says. Since Jesus, however, no longer walks the earth, the Church he founded and its official spokesmen are the ones to be trusted without question.

If you blindly follow what religious authority dictates, you are blessed. You are admirable. You are virtuous.

Oh, what quicksand. What seductive words. That's where the danger comes in. Who doesn't want to be seen as admirable and virtuous? To be so, we are told, just follow us (like sheep).

"Religious" people often see blind belief in religious authority as a holy path. Being a "person of faith" is laudable and its opposite, an infidel, literally a "non-believer," is no doubt the epitome of a degenerate soul.

Many of the same Christians who praise blind belief (faith) often are aghast when others, such as Muslims, do exactly the same.

"Why would they possibly believe the Quran is the final, true revelation by God?"

Answer: they have blind belief in what their religious authorities and their Holy Book say. Just like you.

"But why do they believe Jesus was only a prophet, not God?"

Answer: same as above.

Blind belief in what the leader says is also one of the characteristics of a cult. Granted, cults include other characteristics, such as the crucial one of hindering a person from voluntarily leaving it. But the damage to the individual in terms of independent thinking is similar, whether we speak of a mainstream religion or a cult.

For if authority has the right answers, there is no need to assess both sides of a situation. That has already been done for us. Should we, for example, be opposed to capital punishment? This complex issue can take time and energy to investigate, evaluate, and come to a judgment that fits with our soul. But why waste all that time? Let's just check in with religious authorities and be on our way.

What about the ethics of participating in war? Another highly complicated moral issue. We would serve ourselves well to look at the writings of, indeed, religious figures—in various religions—and also discourses of respected philosophical groups in order to reach the goal of our own conclusions. Thus we can avoid taking on the vacant stare of the stereotypical hypnosis subject who clucks like a chicken, or doesn't, if so bidden.

I myself once drank the Catholic cool-aid laced with the dangerous toxin of blind belief. After indoctrination in Catholic thinking over sixteen years—elementary school, high school, college—I had really believed I possessed the "right answers" via the teachings of the Church. That naivete gradually lessened as I heard the angst of parents with already good-sized families fretting over church rules concerning birth control, or how a family was splintering around the ethical issues of divorce. My solid castle of blind faith crumbled even further in India and Nepal where I rubbed shoulders with sincere people of completely different belief systems, including one highly revered group which didn't believe in a god at all—Buddhists.

I fear that as long as people hold that blind belief is a virtue (but it says so in the Gospel), we will more and more become walking automatons instead of discerning thinkers.

A habit of blind belief eventually hypnotizes the soul.

Community and Ritual
Surely we lose something when we let go of religion and participation in an organized branch of one. The two main losses, I have concluded, are "community and ritual." The loss of a community of like-minded individuals is significant. If we are part of a church, or temple, or similar, we have a ready-made support system at hand, we don't have to search for it. We can count on fellow-members for help in time of spiritual or temporal need. They are there at the ready.

But a tight-knit community can also be suffocating. Should a person step outside the norms of behavior of a particular group—getting a divorce, being gay, having an abortion—the consequences can be harsh. Though being ostracized or shunned may not have the same heavy impact as in days of old, it nevertheless is a sting. All the more so to the extent the person has "bought into" that group heart and soul.

So then, how do we manage if we no longer follow any creed or belong to a special group?

Firstly, we can forge a new view of supportive "community." It doesn't have to be a well-defined group of people who gather every Friday or Saturday or Sunday, as Muslims or Jews or Christians might. It can simply be the loose composite of our circle of friends and family, those people with similar values whose company we enjoy and to whom we turn if we have need.

While value-sharing might often be informal in such a group, it can also take a more structured format when we, secondly, create simple rituals around birthdays, anniversaries, or momentous occasions like marriages or memorial services. And there is no need to limit our rituals to only traditional special events. I have found that people with a wide variety of religious backgrounds appreciate getting together and engaging in rituals during the change of seasons.

"What do you wish will grow in your life in the next several months?" is a question that can elicit in-depth as well as humorous responses during a celebration of Spring. In Fall, one might ask what a person wishes to fade away in their life at this point, or in what way does each one welcome the ever-longer nights?

Resources abound on creating such rituals, and we can freely adapt them to suit ourselves and our gathering.

We are limited in these efforts only by our imagination. And our imaginations are sparked by others who see the value of a group coming together to share important moments and thoughts—the basic components of a community.

Kathmandu and Pokhara, Nepal

"JIM, JIM! OVER here."

An American woman in a sari called to me as I stepped out of Tribhuvan International Airport in Kathmandu. This was my long-time friend Maggie. Originally from Cincinnati, she is married to a Nepali and has lived here for forty years.

We were neighbors back in the 80s, and were often guests at the same gatherings and at each other's homes. One fond memory I have of those years was a weekly gathering at her house, Surya (Sun) Court, where an eclectic gathering of eight of us—Nepali, Indian, American, Austrian—watched and chatted about the BBC series *The Jewel in the Crown*.

Set in the last days of the British Raj, the story is very much about East-West culture clashes, played out against the background of emerging Indian Independence in 1947. What a perfect group we had to view it together. There was no dearth of opinions about the issues and the conversation flowed most easily. Did I mention that Maggie and her husband owned a distillery?

Maggie now lives on the outskirts of Kathmandu in a lovely modern Nepali-style home—red-orange brick, verandahs galore—with six acres of garden, a charming gazebo, and lemon trees to provide a citrus kick to our evening vodka tonics.

Maggie has the scoop on everything. I asked for her assessment of the country in these days of post-monarchy, post-Maoist terrorism days. The look of disgust on her face and her groan said it all. Corruption is on the increase, political infighting doesn't "let things work," and the president is being deferred to and treated like the kings were. In other words, same-same but different.

Yet the Himalayas I see from her back yard are still glorious, almost too much to fully "take in." But definitely not immovable. The Indian Subcontinent's tectonic plate continues to crash into Asia—which is how the Himalayas were created—and cause earthquakes. The one two weeks ago caused a wall to fall at the British Embassy and killed several people. The toll in the countryside is still unclear.

Has Kathmandu changed much since my last visit? Indeed. For better or worse? Yes.

I realize more and more that the writing I've done about my life here thirty years ago is now a "period piece." Arriving by plane in Kathmandu in those days, one first saw the green slopes of the valley, then rice paddies edging right up to the Ring Road, and finally the red brick homes so characteristic of Kathmandu. Kathmandu is built on the floor of an ancient lake, and the clay that lay under those waters has provided plentiful bricks.

Today one first sees boxy, off-white cement buildings well outside the Ring Road and, closer in, stores plastered with advertising over every square centimeter. Urban sprawl is no surprise, but I'm afraid this is just plain junky. Shangri-La has become Shangri-Blah.

On the other hand, electrical power is more consistently delivered to chilly homes in winter. The days of having electricity only every other evening are happily long gone. And cell phones are ubiquitous and so much easier to procure than a land line.

My house had a phone in the 80s but it mainly collected dust since most of my friends didn't have one.

After a few delightful days with Maggie, I headed off to Pokhara, a half hour flight west from Kathmandu, to see Ram, my old friend recently returned from working in Kuwait. As a policeman, his life had been threatened by anti-government Maoist terrorists, but he had escaped Pokhara and was able to get to Kuwait. He worked there for a year and a half, returning for the funeral rituals for his mother. She had already been cremated but Nepali customs call for the main ritual to be held a certain number of days later.

By then the political climate had changed slightly so he stayed back here. With an inheritance from his mother—she owned valuable land in this trekking capital of Nepal—and his Kuwait earnings, he was able to build a good house for his wife and two daughters.

The full moon rose high in the sky over Pokhara, sailing behind clouds in that manner that makes you think it's going some place really quickly. It was Purnima, the last day of the festival of Dashain.

Dashain is a 10-day festival celebrating an ancient myth about the struggle between Good and Evil, where Good eventually wins out. Nepal's calendar is lunar so the festival ends on the full moon, the day I arrived in Pokhara.

I carried envelopes with money in them, a traditional gift, to present to the family on this last day of the festival. I also brought Swiss chocolates.

Ram was grateful and said, "The biggest gift is that you are here. And, you are the eldest so please give us tikka and your blessing when you hand us the envelopes."

And so with the family gathered, I took a pinch of vermillion paste and placed it in the middle of their foreheads. I wished each one good health, long life, and success in achieving their dreams.

Out and About in Pokhara

THE NAMES CHOSEN here for restaurants and hotels never fail to entertain me, and they seem to change rather frequently. Some of my favorites on this trip:

Eat and Fun Restaurant (just what's going on in the backroom?)

Lord Buddha Shopping Corner (good karma if you drop some rupees here)

Bumpkin Cafe

Little Daffodils Boarding School

Lonely Guest House (means it's quiet)

Hotel Bedrock (what are they saying about their mattresses?)

Hungry Feel Restaurant (you feel hungry, you should eat here?)

Future Stars Primary School

...and signs everywhere for Shaka-Laka Boom Boom Noodles

Oh, and the signs attached to Pashmina shawls, "Please Feel Me Dear Human."

I spent the next few days with Ram visiting a holy cave—claustrophobic for me—Goddess Falls, and leisurely roaming around the lake with him on his motorcycle. The motorcycle is basically the family vehicle. No costly car for most families in

Pokhara. If his wife needs to go to the doctor, Ram takes her there on the motorbike. If she is very sick, they take a taxi.

Just a stone's throw from Ram's home is the Royal Guest House, where I have my room. It is pleasant and comes with its own verandah—morning coffee and breakfasts there. The thin door faces west, however, and the afternoon sun beating down increases its warp and requires a determined effort to open between 2 p.m. and 6 p.m.

I was slightly surprised at the name of the guest house. "Royal" has been scrubbed from many a business name since the overthrow of the monarchy. The erstwhile Royal Nepal Airlines is now simply Nepal Airlines. However, "royal" is part of the hotel's website address so perhaps that's why they kept the original name.

On Ram's wife's side, a marriage celebration was being held that week and we all attended the second night of festivities. A power outage temporarily shut down the lighting, so all the motorcycles present lined up on one side of the tent—like cowboys up to the hitching post—to shine their headlights on the party. My bleary eyes were grateful when the power came back.

With electricity came music and dancing, both disco and traditional Nepali folk style. Ram pulled me into the pack and I danced not only to "Sexy Bitch" but also, with all eyes on me according to Ram, to the tunes of traditional Nepali songs. Having watched multiple dance programs in the past and having an ability to imitate, I guess I did all right.

Although Ram complimented me, he in fact was the dance star of the evening. A trained folk dancer in his youth, he still commanded the floor and was the only one who received money stuffed into his pockets, a sure sign of appreciation from other party goers.

The lazy days at lakeside quickly came to an end and the big mechanical bird took me away from a lovely family struggling to improve their lives in a challenging country.

The Basics—Sex and Rice

THE JARDIN RESTAURANT in Kathmandu. Classy. Maggie's Women Entrepreneurs group was having dinner there after several days of planning meetings, and Maggie had asked me to join them since I was her house guest.

Jardin was comfy, had great food, and guess what? It was on my old street just a block from my former home. That neighborhood has become *the* trendy eating place for all of Kathmandu.

Restaurants—French, Italian, upper-end Indian—bistros, tea gardens, nightclubs, and bars are now squeezed in between every two to three houses. It's probably a good thing that the Jardin with its killer cheesecake didn't exist thirty seconds away from my house back then.

The businesswomen's group had brought in a feminist activist from Zimbabwe to facilitate their meetings, and I sat across from her. A fascinating and insightful woman, Hope Chigudu was also planning to lead a discussion on "Sex and Sexuality" the following day.

Whaaat? In this country? A place where of course *everything* happens, but a Culture of Silence shrouds efforts at dealing with sexual issues in a direct and healthy way. After the dinner group dwindled from about twenty to six of us, the discussion turned into a preview of the next day's topic, particularly the differences in various cultures in approaches to sexuality.

Ears perked up and jaws dropped as I explained the work a female friend of mine does as a professional sexual surrogate. The idea that learning about sexuality in a structured and experiential way outside of marriage was acceptable, was news over here. There seems to be an almost universal belief that since sex is a natural urge, we are all somehow equipped to engage in it effectively with practically no instruction at all. I imagine we've all heard sad stories that are a result of such an attitude.

The next day the discussion about sexuality got even livelier as twenty-plus women and men gathered at a private home for the event. You'll have to ask me at another time for details, but the event was definitely a major success. I believe it opened a creaky door to more discussions, and perhaps made a small dent in the literally Fatal Silence here about sexuality.

I spent my last afternoon in Kathmandu with a friend, Dinesh, who is developing a guest house on the eastern slopes of Kathmandu Valley. What a delight to see the place he built himself. He even fired the bricks for the building right there on the property. Pine trees cleanse the air, and bushes of rosemary, thyme, and oregano grant you their scent if you but touch them. Let me know if you'd like to stay there, Lamatar Lodge, a night or two on your next trip to Nepal.

On the way back to Maggie's, we passed fields of rice being harvested the traditional way. Rice stalks are cut, put into small bundles, and then beat on the threshing floor to knock the grain off. Besides the grain, parts of the stalks themselves—the chaff—fall off and are mixed in with the grain. That material is then collected and placed in a plate-like reed pan. The person waits for a slight wind, and lets it all drop down, the air winnowing it—separating the grain from the chaff. The grain is heavier so it drops to the ground and the wind carries away the other refuse.

I have always been charmed when watching the winnowing process, and have also loved the symbolic meaning of the act— getting rid of what is not useful, not digestible. In fact, an early title for my memoir of India and Nepal was *The Winnowing Wind.* I really, really liked that title.

That phrase captured my experience in India and Nepal. Living in those countries had helped me separate the "grain from the chaff" in terms of religious beliefs. But when I had tested that title on others, people either gave me a blank look or asked such odd questions as, "Is that like 'Wind in the Willows'?" or, "Does that have something to do with minnows?" Sheesh, people. I realized I needed a new title.

As I now prepare to leave Nepal after this lovely trip, I realize how blessed I am to have friends here who have so graciously brought me into their circles and into the real charm of any country—meaningful connection with the local people.

The Scribe's Rule

NO, FRIENDS, I don't compose at the computer. I enjoy writing longhand in my notebook at breakfast, in hotel lobbies, or on the verandah at night. Since my time is less structured than someone on an organized tour, I can later get to a computer and rid these ramblings of dangling participles and ambiguous antecedents—at least a lot of them.

The Scribe's Rule: there is no writing, only rewriting.

Hong Kong Interlude

"ESPAÑOL? ESPAÑOL?" THE young, pretty woman just outside Hong Kong Immigration looked at me with pleading eyes. I answered as many of us do, "*Poquito.*" A little.

From Ecuador, she apparently knew not a word of English. In all Asian international airports that I know of, the Arrival Card is printed only in the local language and English. She had filled in only one box, the one marked Sex, probably because that word is a cognate, a word similar in spelling and meaning in two languages.

I helped her fill out the card, and in re-reading it I noticed that she had put M under Sex. I did my best to explain that, no, no, you must write F because M in English stands for *hombre*, and you don't look like that at all. *No pareces como hombre.*

"*Mil gracias,*" a thousand thanks, and she went on her way.

Her choice of M mystified me, and I pondered it to no avail until I was sipping coffee the next morning. Was it because "woman" in Spanish is "*mujer*"? That's my best guess.

Under Sex, I had wanted to put "Sure!" but that could be confusing and perhaps, to some people, unseemly for a newly minted septuagenarian.

At the Immigration booth, I was automatically given a ninety-day visa. While it's not good for mainland China, clearly they want you to spend days on end doing business in Hong Kong.

I had come to Hong Kong from Nepal for my flights to Cambodia and Myanmar. If you, Gentle Readers, happen to twirl that beautiful world globe in your book-lined study, you'll notice I seem to have "overshot" my goal and will have to "go back." But it's all about manipulating cheap fares, free fares, and whatever else I need to.

My flight onward wasn't until the next day, and not wanting to bother going off this island into town, I opted for an airport hotel. $134. I thought that was pretty good for Hong Kong, yes? A Marriott, it was clean and close.

I took in a hot tub soak and a swim in the large pool. The chubby lifeguard—an oxymoron in the U.S.—said it was 27 meters long so I'm guessing 85 feet or so. I was the only one swimming.

The hotel's coffee shop and its lobby, where I write this in longhand, has a view onto the South China Sea. Hong Kong skyscrapers float in the mist across the water. It's definitely an active harbor, with small freighters, ferries, and hovercraft plying the waters in seemingly hazardous crisscross patterns.

Oh. A guy just walked into the lobby with his three little boys, maybe 8, 7, and 6 years old, with leashes attached to their waists and to daddy's belt. They all seemed quite accustomed to this setup and the boys looked happy as magpies. The smallest one was on the shortest leash. Dad, with no other adult companion to help herd the pack, had found a practical solution.

I saw them again later at Immigration and Dad's little troop brought smiles to even those dour Immigration Officers.

Phnom Penh, Cambodia

I ARRIVED IN Phnom Penh with a mixture of anticipation and dread. I looked forward to seeing a city once called the Pearl of Asia, yet knew I could not visit there without being confronted by the horrors perpetrated by the Khmer Rouge in the latter 70s. I imagined I could visit one of the Killing Fields—usually in rural, green areas—but I didn't want to view torture prisons. A TV documentary on Security Prison 21 was as much as I cared to see of that tragedy.

A good friend in the U.S. said S-21 was a globally important place—evidence of the continuing saga of man's inhumanity to man—and that I should just steel myself and visit. Still, I hesitated. Then I discovered that S-21 was across the street from the low-medium hotel I booked. I had to go there.

The dark years.

In 1975 the Khmer Rouge entered the city and sent nearly its entire population to the countryside to work twelve to fifteen-hour days in the rice fields, where many of them died from starvation or disease. The Khmer Rouge wanted a new peasant-based, communist society, and its enemies were those who had participated in the previous societal order. Thus, those speaking French or English, wearing glasses, or being educated were systematically exterminated.

Almost one-third of Cambodia's seven million people perished during this tragic period. How did the country get to this point? Perhaps a bit of history will help enlighten us, but there is sad truth in George Bernard Shaw's quip, "What we learn from history is that we don't learn from history."

Western Colonialization and Local Oppressors

IN NUMEROUS COUNTRIES of South and Southeast Asia, the 19th century brought European colonization. Since those images and a bit of that history is what many Westerners have familiarity with, let's start there.

In 1863, King Norodom of Cambodia fretted that his two neighbors, Vietnam to the east and Siam/Thailand to the west, were prepared to swallow up his country. Seeing an opportunity for themselves, the French strongly "invited" Norodom to make Cambodia a protectorate of France, and Norodom acquiesced.

Now that France had a toehold, it soon expanded its power and rule over the area. By 1887 it had joined Vietnam with Cambodia to form French Indochina, and Laos was added in 1893.

With French rule came French customs, architecture, language, and Christianity. The French, not unlike the British, saw themselves as bearers of beneficial modernization, a highly developed culture, and opportunities for the advancement of the locals. They often said they were on a "civilizing mission," though their own self-interests were what ruled the day.

The Cambodians said, "We already have culture and we don't need your domination and taxes." Protests were to no avail and revolutionaries harshly treated with imprisonment and torture, and sometimes death by guillotine.

Though governmental chaos reigned during WWII in Cambodia, including a period of Japanese domination, at war's conclusion the French once again imposed colonial rule. By 1953, however, they turned the government over to Prince Sihanouk, and Cambodia gained independence.

But trouble began brewing under Sihanouk during the 60s because the North Vietnamese used parts of eastern Cambodia for military bases in its war against the South Vietnamese. The famed Ho Chi Minh Trail, a military supplies route, veered westward from northern Vietnam not only into Laos but also Cambodia, and Sihanouk had made no attempt to flush the northern Vietnamese from his country. This made it appear that Sihanouk was favorable to them, and when he had objected to the U.S. using Cambodian airspace for military purposes this impression was solidified. The U.S. was not happy and bombed those areas of eastern Cambodia known to be North Vietnamese bases.

Sihanouk was ousted by a military coup in 1970, and that same year the monarchy was abolished under the new Khmer Republic. Note: the word *Khmer* refers to a large group of people indigenous to the area as well as Cambodia's current official language.

The Khmer Republic had its own share of infighting, giving rise to various insurgency groups that wanted more drastic changes. These groups included a Communist faction, apparently aided by North Vietnamese, which came to be called the Khmer Rouge, the Red Khmers.

On that fateful New Year's Day in 1975, the Cambodian Communists began their offensive and Phnom Penh fell on April 17, 1975, just five days after the American diplomatic mission abandoned Cambodia. The Khmer Rouge could now "reconstruct" Cambodian society.

The Killing Fields

FOR THOSE IN Phnom Penh destined to take their final life journey to the Killing Fields, the ordeal began with interrogation and torture in S-21, Security Prison 21, which is now Tuol Sleng Museum.

My guide, Maala, was a thirteen-year-old girl in Phnom Penh when the Khmer Rouge took over the city. She was sent to the countryside to work but managed to survive and later be reunited with her mother. She lost her brother, a student, and her father, a professor, though she has no details of what happened to them. Lack of information in this case may actually be a blessing.

The first thing a visitor to Tuol Sleng sees is signs, in Cambodian, French, and English, of the Rules of Behavior for Prisoners, which include the following:

- If you don't follow the rules you shall get many lashes with electric wire.
- If you disobey any regulations you will get either ten lashes or five shocks of electric charge.
- While getting lashes or electrification you must not cry at all.

When the Vietnamese liberated Phnom Penh from the Khmer Rouge in 1979, seven men were found alive in S-21.

Two are still alive today. Their paintings and stories, along with the records the guards kept, detail the atrocities committed in that hellhole.

There are also hundreds of photos on the walls of those poor souls detained there, many showing their final visage after torture. The guards collected this information to show their superiors that the prisoners had not escaped.

I will not describe the faces I saw in the photos, nor the paintings, nor the now-rusted devices of torture. I cannot. And as Maala's monotone voice and stoic face led me through the complex, I wept. I could not find my voice to ask a single question. I looked, and listened, and wept. Even now as I write this, my eyes fill with tears and I can barely see the page I write upon in my notebook.

There are dozens of Killing Fields throughout Cambodia, many still ringed with land mines. Killing Fields are those places characterized by former executions—usually by bludgeoning since bullets were too precious—and mass graves. About nine miles outside of Phnom Penh lies the Killing Field for the thousands of battered humans who arrived there from S-21 for their final fate.

This Killing Field is now a hauntingly serene garden area. The memorial tower in the center holds 8000 skulls, and large depressions in the ground indicate the mass graves. After heavy rains, pieces of bones and teeth work their way up through the soil and are visible today.

Though former detention buildings were torn down by locals needing firewood in the still-bleak days after liberation, audio headsets in various languages enable one to slightly imagine what took place here. And those devices maintain an air of respectful silence in this sad, sad garden.

As Luck Would Have It

"SIR, SIR. I am knowing this place very well." "I drive here the best. You will be very happy with me." "Over here, I am first-class driver!"

From among the tuk-tuk drivers outside my hotel calling to me, I chose a guy named Super Lucky—who always wears an Obama T-shirt, maybe that's why I picked him—to take me around Phnom Penh. A tuk-tuk—pronounced "took took"—is a covered, but open-air vehicle that seats four, driven by a guy on a motorcycle.

Cambodians love the word "lucky." I chatted with a Brit while having lunch yesterday along the Tonle Sap River, and his driver was named Mister Lucky. On my way back to the hotel, I stopped at Lucky Internet, just past the Lucky Guest House, to send my emails. One ubiquitous brand of motorcycle helmets is called Lucky. Let's hope so.

Super Lucky's business card, however, spells his name as Supper Lucky. I will gently coach him on that later.

Louise, a late-fifties Australian staying at my hotel, came up to me during lunch one day, introduced herself, and we chatted away. She is a fount of information. The large number of staff at this place, she explained, is due to the fact that the owner, a Spaniard named Manuel, takes in disadvantaged kids and trains them in the hospitality business in this and his two other hotels. The young men and women are certainly polite, sufficiently versed in English and can switch from riels, the local currency, to dollars and back again with lightning speed, although almost no one negotiates in riels.

All menus and hotel costs are listed in dollars, and ATM's spit out 20-dollar U.S. bills for the asking. Anybody on the street will have dollars. What happened to the good ole Black Market for money exchange?

At 4000 riels to the dollar, I'm glad the menus are in dollars. Who wants to order a six-dollar glass of wine and see a number like 24,000 on the menu?

Louise is here to coach teachers in the villages in more "interactive" ways of engaging the students, instead of the old lecture methods those teachers themselves had been exposed to. She's innovative and adventurous, so no doubt she'll be a hit in the village again. She did this once before.

I invited her to go with me—I'd already hired Super Lucky—to visit the Royal Palace and the adjoining Silver Pagoda. Happily the king wasn't in residence so we got the full royal tour.

Note: in 1993, after years of shaky governments, the monarchy had been reinstated with Sihanouk as king, and the country officially became a constitutional monarchy. The current king is Sihamoni (the eldest son of Sihanouk, who had voluntarily abdicated in 2004).

The Silver Pagoda is a highlight of the palace tour. Built in the 19th century, it received its name from the fact that the floor is composed of silver ingots. The Buddha statues are gold and encrusted with heaps of diamonds, though many statues are covered "only in gold leaf," our guide apologized. I would be a rich man with what I'd carry away under my fingernails if I could get close enough.

The next morning, Super Lucky didn't show up to take me to the bus stand, but luckily for me, hmm, my street is loaded with tuk-tuks, so off I went moments later to my next destination, a bus stand.

The Road to Angkor Wat

I ONCE SAID I'd never do it again, but I just did it and I'm really glad I did, but I'll probably never do it again.

I'm talking about taking an overland bus in Asia when I could take a plane. (I've already had my fill of buses in Asia.) But the six-hour bus trip from Phnom Penh to Siem Reap, the city around which Angkor Wat and many other temples are located, did indeed afford me a view of the countryside I would otherwise have unfortunately missed.

The monsoons are winding down but the effects are still evident. The Mekong and its tributaries have spilt over onto immense floodplains and have submerged rice fields, and flooded homes and businesses.

The fairly decent two-lane paved road zips along a three-foot high "causeway" through the area. In some places, water stretches out to your right and left as far as the eye can see, but the illusion of being in the middle of a lake is dispelled by the tree tops scattered throughout, the temples isolated on small mounds of earth, and the lines of pilgrims treading through knee-deep water to reach the shrines.

Most houses near the road are built on stilts but need rickety bamboo walkways for access. One carefree group of folks we passed sat on chairs in front of a restaurant with water up to mid-calf, enjoying their tea and chatting happily away.

Upon arrival in Siem Reap, my tuk-tuk driver Raman, recommended by a friend, awaited me with my name on a sign and a smile on his face. A young man of perhaps twenty years, a slight build and perfectly smooth complexion, he did not sport a bubbly personality but seemed quite intent that I have a good visit. "We shall see the most important places here. You will like them very much."

Off we went to the Mekong Boutique Hotel to make plans for the morrow. I was slightly disappointed and a bit perplexed when Raman told me we couldn't go to the famous "floating village" I wanted to see because it had been flooded. Huh? Wouldn't flooding kinda help?

Cuius Regio, Eius Religio

"WHOSE REALM, HIS religion."
The first time I'd seen a picture of or even heard of Angkor Wat
was in the late 60s. This was Cambodia's Golden Period, the time
between independence from France in 1953 and the tragedy of
the Khmer Rouge in the 70s. The picture was of Jackie Kennedy
posing in front of a mysterious temple which was octopussed by
long, searching tree roots.

Since then, those temple images have quietly lurked in my
mind, not insisting on a visit but gently inviting.

Here I am.

"Angkor" means capital city or holy city and there are multiple such complexes within a short distance of the city of Siem
Reap. The Cambodian Empire had once stretched out broad-
ly, including significant parts of its now-neighboring countries.
Siem Reap in fact means "Victory over Siam," that is, Thailand.

Cambodia's history is dotted with wars and revolutions, and
each new king's ego often demanded a new venue for his creative
ambition and spiritual devotion. Thus, the many temple-capitals
around Siem Reap. The complex specifically known as Angkor
Wat, 12th century, is the largest of these capitals and the best
preserved since it was never totally abandoned to the jungle.

While London in those days may have had a population of 18,000, Angkor Wat had about one million inhabitants—easily the largest city in the world until the Industrial Revolution. The wooden homes of the commoners are long gone of course.

With a change of king often came a change in the official religion, which kept swinging from Hinduism to Buddhism and back and forth several times. Large walls of a complex, with dozens of Buddha statues having been knocked down, now show lotus pads sitting there quite empty.

"Your parents' religion, your religion."
Kings and other rulers presumably no longer force their subjects into embracing their own religion, but the king and queen of our little family realm—our parents—usually brought us up in their religion. No doubt there are many exceptions, but that is the most common pattern.

What we might profess as "deep faith" is really deep conditioning. It's what we are brought up with, what we are accustomed to hearing, what may sound to us like Ultimate Truth. That certainly was the case for me during the first half of my life. With parents of Irish, Polish, and French backgrounds, Catholicism was the only item on the religion menu. I gobbled it all up, with my allegiance to its precepts reinforced by attending Catholic elementary school, Catholic high school, and then joining the Brotherhood.

I wasn't familiar with any other religious tradition. A few kids in my childhood neighborhood were from Protestant families, but I understood they were simply less fortunate than I who had been blessed with the One, Holy, Catholic, and Apostolic Faith. They were, however, at least Christians.

Not until I lived in Delhi in my late thirties did I give serious thought to how we come to believe what we believe. The Hindu across the street was carrying on the traditions of his parents. The Muslim around the corner was doing the same thing, as was the Jain farther down the street. And I was reciting morning prayers to my guardian angel and attending Mass regularly, as had my parents.

A fish doesn't know it's in water.

So, what we carry in our hearts and souls as important, true, and sometimes even worthy of dying for has nothing to do with "objective truth" but rather *is mainly a function of which family we were born into.*

And that early religious rooting definitely served both as an anchor in a secularist society and as a beacon for moral behavior. Can we do without such?

When, years ago, after reflecting on my experiences in India and Nepal, I had decided not only to leave the Brotherhood, but the Church and Christianity as well, the most frequent question from friends was not about where I would live or what profession I would pursue. It was about religion itself.

"But what have you *replaced* it with?" inquiring minds asked about the surely unnatural vacuum I had created. Are you a Buddhist or a Hindu now, they asked. Why go from the frying pan into the fire, I said, and replace one set of arbitrary beliefs with another.

The radical practices of Christianity—such as love your enemies and go the extra mile—I still carry with me and aim to live out. One can strive for that without professing belief in a Trinity or a Virgin Birth or Original Sin.

Those empty temple lotus pads, I have come to think, were not "missing something." A space had been created for viewpoints and practices far broader than had been encompassed by the original icons.

Yesterday I visited Ta Phrom before going to Angkor Wat, borne there on a tuk-tuk with Raman both as driver and tour guide. Ta Phrom is the least restored of the temples, and therefore sports many of those magnificent gnarly trees in front of which everyone wants to be photographed. I may have more pictures of darting Japanese tourists—who move in large chattering packs—than I have of the fabulous trees. The most popular photo-op is with the tree featured in an Angelina Jolie/Lara Croft movie.

Happily it has been decided not to restore the walls and temples that are crumbling in Ta Phrom due to the very popular trees. I'm sure that was actually not an easy decision for the historically minded. Those trees are the "enemies" of the temples. Do you want temples restored to their original look, or temples continuing to crumble because of the trees? No one asked me, but I'd vote to preserve the trees. This place has enough other restored temples to satisfy even the most insatiable archeologist, I would think.

The above was Day 2. Day 1 was less happy.

Although the temples I visited that first day were breath-taking, so was the heat. I also had a stomach ache from who-knows-what, and leg pain that I've had in the past had revisited me. For clothing I thought shorts and sandals would be cool, but the sandals gave little support for going up steep steps and navigating high temple thresholds. Combine those sandals and the leg pain, and I looked like an old man wondering where his cane was. Oh.

The pockets in the shorts were overly baggy and, traveler's nightmare, my wallet containing cash, my credit card and ATM card fell out somewhere. Gone.

Terrible feeling in the stomach, a police report, and a very sympathetic Raman were the next events. However, I had money wired to me here and my now closely guarded new wallet is fat with greenbacks (actually, the bills are multi-colored notes here). In a few days I leave for Myanmar where credit cards and traveler's checks cannot be used anyway. But there is still something missing—the security, or its illusion, that comes with having plastic in your pocket that boasts a $10,000 reservoir.

The Local Scene

PLEASE DON'T DRINK the Pepsi
The sign says "Cold Drinks" but they're not cold and the cases are stacked outside the many small open-front shops that line the streets. Right next to piles of Coke and Orange Fanta are liter-size Pepsi bottles that contain a light amber-colored fluid. The other day when my sputtering tuk-tuk pulled over to one of those stores, the shopkeeper immediately came forward with a Pepsi bottle to solve the fuel issue. Right, that's gasoline in those Pepsi bottles, baking away in the sun.

"Fish Massage, No Piranhas"
Under this sign, two British guys sat with their feet submerged in a large aquarium with small fish darting around. The watery creatures gently nibble on your feet, chomping up dead skin, and it's listed as the best pedicure in town. One Brit said it was kinda cool and urged me to put my hand inside. I did. Mainly it was ticklish. I moved on.

Nighttime Food Courts
Khmer food. Love it. A bit like Thai, but with unique spices and flavors which are definitely new for me. I intend to seek out Cambodian restaurants when I return to the U.S.

The evening food courts I frequented are on a school playground which morphs at night into a bustling circus of the senses. Caldrons of soup simmer next to fish grilling on an open fire, woks get their contents flipped by dexterous cooks, and a woman squats to fan a charcoal fire—sparks flying into the night like those spider-fireworks—under a pot that is cooking jasmine rice.

I've gone there several times with Raman who is keen on my having good food and getting it at a bargain rate. Poor Raman, I think he stressed over my loss of the credit and debit cards almost as much as I. This is because by local custom he is supposed to take care of "his" tourist and not let untoward things happen to me. I have assured him many times that it was I who was careless, and that I would be ok.

Unfortunately the hotel receptionist chided him and said he must always ask me if I have my camera and wallet every time we are ready to leave a temple area. He does this now in a totally charming way.

Raman is new at being a tour guide and has asked for my feedback to help him improve. I make sure I congratulate him first on a "very fine job" and then I have him practice the pronunciation of certain words he used that I would not have recognized had I not read the guidebook ahead of time. His pronunciation of "Sacred Sword," the name of one temple, was totally incomprehensible to me.

He diligently repeats after me and is genuinely grateful. He wants to attend college and take courses in English, but the other night his English course was canceled for the third time this fall because of insufficient student enrollment. He will see what happens next week. I will definitely "overpay" this young man.

Golden

Besides "lucky," "golden" is another favorite word here. You can always find a Golden Dragon Guest House, or a Gold Lotus Bar, or a Golden Sunrise whatever.

I discovered another "Golden" the other day.

Backtrack first. On the bus to Siem Reap several days ago, I noticed a gay couple a few rows behind me on the other side of the bus. One guy was a forty-something Anglo and the other a twenty-something Cambodian, holding hands the whole trip, both of them aglow. It wasn't difficult to get the picture.

Then the other night, after Raman and I had eaten dinner and he left for his home, I walked around nearby Bar Street—just what it sounds like—and heard someone calling, "Hello, hello!" from a sidewalk bar. It was the couple from the bus, Frank an Aussie, and Pally a Cambodian. They invited me to have a drink with them in that gay bar, called Linga. Well, hello...

While chatting about our various backgrounds and what we were seeing in Siem Reap, they mentioned that their hotel had a pool. The first day I arrived here, I wished I had asked Raman to book me into a hotel with that amenity.

"Come on over for a swim. We're staying at a cool gay hotel called the Golden Banana."

I kid you not.

Before leaving for a night swim at the Golden Banana, my attention drifted back to a serious-looking, middle-aged Western woman alone at the next table. For some time, she had been staring into her clear drink, head bowed.

"Is that vodka? Do you like it?" I ventured.

Miss Stone Face transformed into a vivacious and engaging Canadian who had just completed three years of teaching English in Korea and was vacationing before her next gig teaching

English in Laos, "Pronounced *Lao* you know." A former bartender, Evelyn also gave me more secret tips—"It must be vodka *l'orange*, of course"—than I'll ever remember.

The interesting people you can meet, everywhere. And I suspect there are many folks like Evelyn—like myself sometimes—who only need a little encouragement or invitation to open up. That is a gift we can easily provide to fellow-travelers anywhere on this planet.

* * *

Departure

I had paid Raman in the afternoon of my last day in Siem Reap. When he came to pick me up for the airport in the evening, the first thing he did—after asking how I was doing—was to proudly show me a receipt for the tuition he owed for this semester's classes.

He wanted me to know how he had spent the money I gave him. Bless that young man.

Yangon, Myanmar

"IF YOU SEE only one stupa in Southeast Asia, let it be Shwedagon in Yangon," the guidebook says. I couldn't agree more.

A stupa is a mound-shaped Buddhist shrine, and this fabled one rises high enough to be seen from any part of the city. It is the pride and joy and heart of Yangon (formerly Rangoon, Burma). While most historians and archeologists maintain that the stupa was built between the 6th and 10th centuries C.E., legend says it was built 2600 years ago and contains several important relics, including eight hairs of Gautama Buddha. (For all the hairs of the Buddha that you can supposedly encounter in reliquaries across Asia, he must have been exceedingly hirsute.)

The stupa's heritage certainly is rich and its layers of gold real. Kings and queens for centuries have donated their weight in gold to create this dazzling sight. The highest point, about 330 feet, contains 5000 diamonds—one of them at 76 carats—and an additional 2000+ precious gems.

Visiting Shwedagon was the one time in all my travels I wished I had worn sunglasses, no joke. The shining gold in such great mass is painful to the unguarded eyes. I literally, physically gasped each time I turned a corner and got a new view of the stupa or its 82 outer structures. The additional structures are stunning in themselves—silver, gold, white marble, glass mosaic—housing hundreds of Buddha statues in meditation pose as well as a few in reclining position.

Very importantly and significantly, this is a real live place of devotion. No beguiling ruins, these structures. Monks and lay folk are seen everywhere lighting incense, presenting flowers, pouring blessed water over statues, or bowing low in reverence. An air of quiet respect pervades this temple.

What are not seen are large tour groups. A good number of tourists are here, but mainly as individuals, couples, threes or fours, rather blending in—except for us Westerners' skin color. Now, I myself have been a member of a large touring group at times and I do not disparage that mode of travel. But the fact is that such numbers, with a tour guide shouting explanations from the front and waving a distinctive handkerchief, decidedly change the atmosphere and no venue more unfortunately so than a place of devotion.

The day will probably come when non-devotees taking tons of photos—as I did—outnumber the pious, so go see Shwedagon now.

Miss Lily, my soft-spoken guide, invited me to partake in several of the shrine rituals, including the pouring of blessed water on Buddha statues. From her handy-dandy little book, she determined I was born on a Sunday, and led me to the appropriate place for the ablutions. As we passed the shrine for those born on Saturday, I expected Sunday's altar to be next. But the "order" here for the statues is not according to the days of the week but rather that of the position of the planets from the sun. Love that.

The planets' position in relation to the sun is remembered by this pneumonic: My Very Educated Mother Just Served Us Nine

Pizzas. Mercury, Venus, Earth (third rock from the sun), Mars, Jupiter, Saturn, Uranus, Neptune, and Pluto.

(The "planets" visible to the naked eye have for millennia named the days of the week in this order: Sun, Moon, Mars, Mercury, Jupiter, Venus, and Saturn. The Spanish and French names for the days of the week may help you see the correlation a bit better than the English names.)

Buddhist devotees at Sunday's shrine smiled and welcomed me as I poured water first over Garuda, protector, then over Buddha as man, then Buddha as enlightened man. Recall, Buddha is not a "god," simply a man who "attained" freedom from anguish.

At another shrine, one makes a wish and then lifts a rather heavy stone. You are asked to be more humble and sincere, and lift it again. When/if the stone feels lighter, the wish will come true. I swear to Buddha that the stone felt lighter on my third try but I cannot remember what I wished for.

After my tour with Miss Lily—who, like most Burmese women, wears sandalwood paste on her face as both makeup and sunscreen—had ended, I stayed on a bit to further "absorb" the place. A spot on cool marble steps seemed to beckon me.

After several minutes, a young monk with shaven head and saffron robe came to where I sat and very gently placed himself quite close to me, our elbows touching.

He said nothing, just looked at me with wide eyes. I smiled, and he smiled back. I asked, "How are you?" and his response, consisting of movements, seemed to indicate that he was deaf.

We sat quietly.

Later I motioned to my camera. He shook his head no. My own non-Buddhist desire *so* wanted a photo to remember that beautiful, serene face. We sat silently next to each other awhile, then I made a move to leave. We nodded to each other and, like the fleetingness of a prayer flag's position in the wind, our connection was over.

Or is it?

Lobby of the Strand Hotel

This posh, steamship-era hotel recalls the days when shipping magnates ruled the roost and the elite met here near the river for Afternoon Tea at 4 p.m. Oversized wicker chairs and settees still dominate the decor, and the dark wood of the adjacent bar smells more than faintly of the untold number of cigars smoked there at one time.

"Posh" has often been described as an acronym for "port out, starboard home," referring to the days when Brits traveled to Asia on passenger boats. The preferred staterooms would have been on the cooler, more northerly side of the ship, that is, left/port going out, and starboard/right, going home. I was once completely enamored of this trivia but it is disappointingly quite apocryphal.

I was having a late-afternoon pick-me-up latte here at the Strand after a self-guided tour of the—rather rundown I'd say—downtown area. I've discovered that the black market for money exchange is definitely vibrant here. I just shake my head no and walk on. It's too risky.

After that refreshing caffeinated interlude, I picked my way back to my hotel along dark, though supposedly safe, streets and ruptured sidewalks alive with thousands of Burmese having dinner in the open. They sit on small plastic chairs, maybe ten inches off the ground, around a low table—all of which looks like a child's tea set arrangement. Somewhere nearby their dinner cooks over an open brazier and they eat it in total darkness, save for the intermittent flash of car headlights.

Amidst this shadowy scene, I spied the Monsoon Restaurant, a name I recognized from the guidebook. I entered and found myself in an elegant oasis—an old colonial building with fifteen-foot ceilings, whirring fans overhead, white columns supporting the large dining area, spotless ivory tablecloths throughout, and the subdued lighting of a supper club. I immediately relaxed.

Scouring the menu, I debated between choosing the Chicken Satay or the Mushrooms with Ginger, the latter of which sounded tasty but not even vaguely substantial. When I asked the waiter for his opinion, he replied that the chicken was only four pieces of meat but that the mushroom dish would be a good meal for me.

"That one comes with rice."

There is a saying in many parts of Asia, "If you haven't had rice today, you haven't eaten today."

I ordered the Mushrooms with Ginger, and enjoyed it with rice.

After dinner, I lingered in the comfortable restaurant and pulled out a book from my shoulder bag to read. It's the one book in English you are certain to find in almost every gift shop and souvenir store in Myanmar: George Orwell's scathing 1934 portrait of corruption and imperial bigotry in British-ruled Burma, *Burmese Days*.

The British and Other Scoundrels in Burma

WHILE I SHALL briefly report on the major oppressors of Burma in the 19th and 20th centuries, I am not ignorant of the previous foreign invasions, bloody civil wars, and ruthless local kings whose stories populate almost any country's history. I leave that narrative to others.

During the political instability in the 19th century created by warring independent Burmese states, an expansionist British government stepped in, fought three Anglo-Burmese wars over a period of 60 years, and finally annexed Burma as part of its Empire in 1886. Most accounts of British rule in Burma emphasize that it furthered divisions between local groups by favoring some ethnic minorities over others. With such animosity between locals, the country has had one of the longest running civil wars of almost any nation, enduring even to today.

Open resistance to British rule began to appear sporadically during the 1920s. Later in 1935 a law student, Aung San, organized strikes at Rangoon University to bring visibility to a growing independence movement. As the strikes continued Aung San made a name for himself and gained the support of the nation.

Although Aung San initially supported the Japanese in World War II—a fact emphasized by his detractors—because they promised Burmese independence, he soon saw that as an empty promise and switched allegiance to the British war effort. After the war Aung San, whose party had swept the elections for the Constituent Assembly, began negotiations with the British for full Burmese independence.

In July 1947, Aung San sat in amiable though stimulating conversation with several of his ministers in the immense Secretariat Building—currently called the Ministers Building—in central Rangoon, drafting a new constitution. The Victorian structure, constructed of red and yellow brick and covering a full city block, was the administrative seat of British Burma. The edifice awed locals in those days and still does.

That morning's deliberations were interrupted as members of an opposition party burst into the room with machine guns and, bullets spewing in all directions, assassinated Aung San and six of his cabinet ministers. Aung San was 32 years old. The nation was in shock.

The perpetrators were eventually brought to justice and independence was granted to Burma on January 4, 1948, with another member of Aung San's cabinet at the helm. The specific time chosen for Independence was 4:20 a.m., an hour the astrologers deemed auspicious.

For the next ten years, however, political instability ruled the day as many insurgent groups—believing they were underrepresented in the constitution—created civil war and widespread unrest. In 1958 General Ne Win took over the country in order to "establish law and order" and solidified his position as the country's military dictator by 1962. Although Burma had recently begun an economic upswing, the nation now tumbled into cultural, environmental, and economic ruin.

When, in July 1988, Ne Win indicated he was stepping aside, thousands of jubilant Burmese took to the streets and held demonstrations during the so-called "Democracy Summer." But in August army troops began firing on the people, killing at least 10,000 demonstrators across the country. International condemnation quickly followed.

By a remarkable coincidence that very year—some philosophies state that "there are no coincidences"—a middle-aged woman of Burmese origin who had been living abroad for some years had returned to the country to care for her ill mother. Married to a Brit and mother of two sons, her previous fifteen years had been spent mainly in England. Now she was back and in the midst of Burmese political turmoil. Her studies and work abroad had primarily been in the field of politics, and she soon came to the attention of pro-democracy groups.

Her name was Aung San Suu Kyi, youngest daughter of Aung San, the Father of Burmese Independence.

As head of the newly formed National League for Democracy, she became a lightning rod for government oppression and spent the next fifteen of twenty-one years under house arrest. Her party won over 80% of the legislative seats in the election of 1990 but the military junta, surprised and outraged, refused to seat them and nullified the election.

That same year she was awarded the Nobel Peace Prize though she was not permitted to leave the country to accept it. Her sons received the honor in her place and she used the prize money to establish a health and education trust for the

Burmese people. At various times during her house arrest, she would have been granted permission to travel abroad to see her husband and sons but only on the condition that she never return to Burma. She refused such conditions, stating that many imprisoned patriots could not see their loved ones, many of whom didn't have the security and comfort her family abroad enjoyed.

At this writing, Aung San Suu Kyi's role and influence in Burmese politics is uncertain, though international observers believe she will soon likely have a key role in government.

Bagan and the Field of 4400 Temples

LUSH GREEN FIELDS stretch out in every direction around Bagan, three hundred miles north of Yangon. Now I collect the benefits of arriving here just as the rains have finished. It's still humid but the normally dry central plain of Myanmar, upon which rest some 4400 stupas/temples, is dusty no more, at least for a few months.

Bagan, formerly Pagan, is the seat of the 11th century Pagan Empire, the first unification of the various regions that would later become modern day Burma. But its real attraction for today's traveler is the striking scene of those many temples lining the horizon.

While Yangon's Shwedagon pagoda is still a major highlight of this trip, I am happy to leave that city: shabby and rundown, black water stains traveling twenty to thirty feet down cement buildings, and no charming "riverfront" area as in Phnom Penh, even though Yangon is bordered by two rivers. I know Yangon was battered by a damaging typhoon in 2008, but much of the decay looks rather long term.

I feel for the people of Myanmar. They have surely been through a lot in the past few decades politically, and now even their main city suffers. The generals moved the official capital away from Yangon in 2005 because of advice from astrologers. While there is supposedly less focus now on "correct thinking" in Yangon, the government also took much-needed revenue with them.

The people here seem a bit shyer than in Cambodia, not as engaging at first, and more serious. But they are genuinely lovely and polite, and even the vendors are not pushy. The reticence I perceive may be a result of autocratic kings for centuries, colonialism, a fleeting grasp at democracy, and a military regime at the moment.

Myanmar has been ostracized by the official international community because of the regime's poor record on human rights. This "distancing" is understandable and well-intentioned. But who really suffers? The generals? I doubt it.

My hotel is lovely. It's located in New Bagan with middle level hotels, as opposed to Old Bagan with four and five-star hotels or Nyaung-U with budget range hotels. The Hotel Kumudara, Lotus Flower, is situated on several green acres surrounded by temples and farms. It has a 45-ft swimming pool, views of the temples from my balcony, air-conditioning in the rooms, and free though slow internet. The covered but open-air restaurant on a huge wooden deck where I write in my notebook has become "my spot."

This evening I went to the pool. The sky sparkled with stars, and the sounds of the crickets were incessant. I was careful not to walk on the lawn because of the frogs, which are legion and make me think of a biblical plague. Remember, this hotel borders on farms, so no fences here. Earlier during my afternoon swim, a local farmer pastured a herd of goats perhaps 75 feet from the pool, no fence separating us.

The water in the pool here, as at the Golden Banana, is salt water though neither locale is anywhere near the ocean. I'm guessing that the salt substitutes for chorine, which I do not smell at all, as a disinfectant.

In my spare time—it's all spare time here for me—I read. I slowly turn the pages of Orwell's *Burmese Days*—locally printed on cheap and yellowing paper—and am quite taken by how unblinkingly the author addresses racism and opportunism, both foundations of British colonialism. He was considered by many to be a traitor to the homeland in those days. Remember, the Raj was still raging in the 1930s. I won't say more about the book. Please read it.

Words, Language, Politics—Sheesh!

ETYMOLOGY—THE STUDY OF the origin of words—is, I have concluded, a patchwork of research, conjecture, error, and more conjecture. Nevertheless I plunge ahead where angels hesitate to place their nonexistent feet and offer you the following.

"Burma" or "Myanmar"? Isn't it caving in to those self-serving generals who renamed the country in 1989, a year after those terrible massacres, to call it Myanmar? Not so fast.

It turns out that the Burmese language is not only "tonal"—a completely intimidating concept to me—but also has "register." Who knew? "Register" means that different words for the same idea/thing are used depending on the social context. A simple cousin of this concept would be the use of the pronoun "you" in languages like French, Spanish, Hindi, and no doubt others. A different word for "you" is used depending upon the social status of the speaker in relation to that of the person spoken to.

Historically, the Burmese nation itself has long been referred to by the locals as Burma in speech—spoken register—but as Myanmar in formal writing, considered literary register. And even these names are derivations/adaptations/corruptions of earlier forms of those words.

The word Burma likely comes from the largest of the ethnic groups that settled in the central plains in the 7th century, the Bamars, or Bamas, and whose language is the origin of modern-day Burmese.

Yet, inconsistency abounds. Rangoon was changed to Yangon to reflect the fact that "r" is no longer used in Standard Burmese. However, even though the formal name in Burmese for the country is closer to *Myanma*, its official name in English became Myanmar, with that "r" in there. Go figure.

The 1989 commission on English names thought Myanmar would sound more inclusive than Burma, especially to non-Bamar ethnicities—a laudable idea in itself—though that too is disputed by some minorities.

I won't be trying to learn Burmese.

Temple Hopping and Money Matters

AFTER THE SHWEDAGON in Yangon why see more stupas, like the 4400 such in Bagan?

Think of the rows upon rows of headstones in Arlington Cemetery or in the WWII cemetery in Normandy, France. Those images convey a sense of the human cost of war at a scale that a single grave, even the poignant Tomb of the Unknown Soldier, cannot give.

In a similar vein, thousands of temples strewn out before the eye, some with golden domes glittering in the sun, are a particularly powerful statement about the determination to continually acknowledge something greater than the self. Unlike the mixture of Hindu and Buddhist shrines of Angkor, these temples are solely Buddhist and most are living places of devotion today.

Built between the 11th and 13th centuries, these stupas could in part be seen as the ego statements of certain kings. But the towering Buddha statues and carefully wrought engravings inside the temples, and the candles placed before the images remind me of the importance of taking time with the major questions of life. Who am I? What is my purpose? What indeed is this "I"? Being forced to look at such important matters is a gift of this most unusual place.

I ponder these questions, especially at dusk, and suspect the "answer" is elusive but I must seek after it nevertheless.

Lao Tzu, a Chinese contemporary of the Buddha, had a thought about the great Truths, similar to the Buddha's answer in the Flower Sermon. In his day, 6th century BCE, he was well-known as a spiritual teacher, and the Emperor had even asked him to reside at court. But Lao Tzu understood that he who eats the ruler's bread must mouth the ruler's policies, and so he refused. Legend says that toward the end of his life, he set out on a donkey to spend the rest of his days in the quiet environs of the frontier lands. At the border a guard recognized him and would not let him pass until he had written down his wisdom. Lao Tzu—which means Revered Elder—spent the next three days in a simple hut and wrote the Tao Te Ching, the classic text of Taoism.

"The Tao (great truth, reality, the way) that can be uttered is not the eternal Tao." Thus begins this classic book. Once again, we are reminded that our words are but sorry attempts at describing reality. The 13th century Persian poet Rumi said, "Language is a tailor's shop where nothing fits." When will we stop expecting others to accept our descriptions of the unseen?

On this trip I am reading a book of essays by contemporary Buddhist teachers who keep these questions alive for me and help turn the stone temples before me into occasions of meditation.

Favorite true story I read today:

An American woman who had been living in India for two years was having tea one day with the lama when a fly fell into her teacup. She thought she was unperturbed and more "Buddhist" by now concerning such things, but a look of dismay must have crossed her face for the lama's eighteen-year-old apprentice asked her what was the matter. She told him about the fly but assured him it was no problem.

"Oh, a fly in the tea," he repeated several times, then put his finger into the cup and removed the intruder.

"Really, it's all right," the woman assured him.

A few minutes later the apprentice returned beaming, "Yes, it's going to be all right."

Back to the Black (Market)

My last day in Bagan began with stress over money, again. I had plenty of cash but the hotel staff is positively anal about not accepting U.S. dollars which have a crease in them. I'm not talking worn and torn and tattered. I'm talking a faint line. They hold the bill up to the light and if a hint of a crease can be observed they ask for a different one. Do they think we arrived here straight from the U.S. mint? Later I learned that Burma exchanges these dollars with the Chinese, who are quite particular about their condition.

I'm sure the front desk girl was just doing as instructed when she declined my cash, but I then realized with a sinking feeling that I was now fresh out of crispies. My remaining hundreds of dollars all had creases in them and I was leaving the next day for my last stop, Inle Lake. If no one would accept my wrinkles—we're talking cash bills here—how would I pay for hotel, taxi, and food?

I wrestled with the problem for quite a while until I realized the obvious. I don't have to figure this out. Someone *else* will solve this situation for me. Someone will appear, or is already here, who can guide me. An angel, as it were.

So, who would that be? Oh, who at this hotel knows seemingly everything: local events, the hotel history, which tour groups are coming and going, what small pagodas to visit and which shops to patronize—including his brother's veggie diner, Be Kind to Animals Restaurant, and his auntie's lacquer store? Zaw Zaw.

Zaw Zaw is the restaurant manager and no doubt spends more time with each guest than any other staff member, helping us in various ways. Twice in fact he has drawn helpful little maps for me on table napkins.

I told Zaw Zaw my situation and he gave the answer we all love to hear. "No problem, I know somebody."

Later, I climbed onto the back of his motorbike and off we went down dirt roads, past the high school his son attends, and eventually pulled up in front of a simple house. We entered by the side gate and walked down the narrow mud area to the back of the house. A stylish young woman beckoned us to enter and gestured toward an older, dignified woman with fingers draped over a large cash box.

Via translation from Zaw Zaw and with her calculator, she let me know that the exchange rate would be 730 kyats—local currency, pronounced "jets"—to the dollar, better than the 700 at the hotel. Great. I had been prepared to take less than 700 if only someone would accept my imperfect cash.

The money was carefully counted out by her, then by me, and again by Zaw Zaw. All was in order. This was not a fast and furtive exchange in the bazaar where one can be taken in. My fear of being taken advantage of in the bazaar had precluded my considering that the answer was in the black market.

I was surprised that my less-than-mint-condition bills would be accepted. Zaw Zaw explained that the black market folks knew how to wet the bills and flatten them properly, then in turn get 850–900 kyats per dollar for themselves. I gave him a nice fat "cut." Now he, I, and the money lady are all happy. Win-Win-Win.

Inle Lake

IMAGINE CRATER LAKE or Lake Tahoe where the hills run straight down to the lake, precluding the existence of much flat land at water's edge. Thus it is with Inle Lake, and therefore the airport is in the hills some twenty miles away. A taxi drove me down to the lake where I boarded a boat to reach my hotel.

An oblong body of water, the lake lies at the edge of mysterious Shan territory, a hilly, misty home of many proud tribes, the inner areas of which are forbidden to foreigners because of revolutionaries 'lurking in them thar hills.'

For a mesmerizing story about this area in the 19th century, read *The Piano Tuner* by Daniel Mason. The protagonist is a nose-to-the-grindstone, flat-affect Londoner who specializes in a certain type of piano. He receives a request/summons to travel to Burma because a high-level British officer's piano has—surprise, surprise—gone out of tune in the humid tropics of remote Shan territory. Read on from there...

Inle Lake is a live, pulsating community of farmers, artisans, and metal workers who live and work on the lake. Take the word "on" literally. Whole villages lie offshore, raised above the water on stilts.

My hotel, Golden Island Cottages, is also an off-shore stilted mini-village of staff, visitors, and boatmen plying their trade. The cottages are linked by raised sidewalks, and arched bridges take you to the main reception area and dining room. No air-conditioning is needed here in this cool environment at 3000 feet.

In late afternoon I headed toward the dining room for refreshment. I had been musing to myself since my arrival that, as much as I enjoy traveling alone, a magical setting such as this would be a great place to socialize with others.

A Western couple sat on the deck of the dining room admiring the sunset, a bottle of wine shining ruby-red in the slant rays of the sun. I stopped to take a picture of the scene and had just started to say, "You guys know how to do it," when the woman turned toward me and we recognized each other.

Remember my telling you a few weeks ago about a discussion on Sexuality in Kathmandu? Kathy, an American who works several months each year at a children's home in Kathmandu had attended that discussion. Afterwards we had chatted, discovered we were both going to Myanmar eventually, and said wouldn't it be fun if we ran into each other.

Well, here she was with her husband Tony. As you can imagine, that meeting led to stimulating conversations, sharing a table at breakfast and dinner, and happily running into each other as our respective tour guides took us to the same sight-seeing places.

Tony had researched Myanmar extensively and planned out a several week tour for them. He also totes a long-nosed camera and admits to shooting everything in sight from several angles. Kathy just smiles. Married for thirty-five years, they know each other's ways.

Kathy, like me, has seen Kathmandu change much over the years and also finds the place rather exhausting these days. But her work at the children's home is important to her and is also, I would guess, a helpful catalyst for her own "inner" work according to a conversation we had at dinner the other night. She recounted a dream she'd had about Nepal and certainly "had that been my dream" it would be in part about how Nepal figured into my own soul's journey. She resonated with much of my projection. Dreams are truly a universal language of the soul.

Around Inle Lake
My boat guy, with red-stained teeth from years of chewing betel nut—which occurs here in epidemic scale—zipped the boat out through the hotel's harbor and headed toward the popular morning market.

The boat is what I'd call a "long boat" or "war canoe," narrow and long enough for four or five people to sit single file on low chairs. A noisy motor churns up a small wake and lets you slice through the water.

At least two dozen such boats had tied up at the market, situated on a rare piece of soggy shore land. The first stalls are souvenirs and trinkets for tourists, but if you wander farther in you spy what the locals are choosing from: burlap bags of rice, reed baskets of transparent noodles, tomatoes, dried fish tied in bundles, crimson chilies, piles of eggs, and more. Food stalls wok up tiny battered fish and omelets which are laced with green, red, and orange chilies. I wouldn't touch those chili-laden eggs but they are met with smiles by hungry locals.

I bought a burgundy-colored *longyi*, which is a sarong-like wraparound for men. I've worn similar such in India many times, much cooler in hot weather than pants that choke off airflow around your legs.

As we cruised the main waterways of several stilted villages, locals ferried smaller cargo from place to place on their silent, gliding canoes, and larger loads—such as "seaweed" or bottled water or gasoline—on powered craft similar to the tour boats.

Seaweed? Or perhaps peat moss or similar, pulled up from the lake. This is used to provide a nutrient base for the floating gardens. Right now the main crop growing on those water-borne patches is tomatoes, though rows of cauliflower can also be seen. Long bamboo poles thrust down into the lake's mud anchor the buoyant clumps to one spot. At this time, after the rainy season, the water is about 25 feet deep.

My boat nestled up against one of the floaters not yet plant-ed, and I gingerly stepped out onto it. Yeah, a little crazy. My feet sank into water but only just above the ankles. I clung to the anchoring bamboo for balance while Boat Guy snapped a photo.

A squall came up midafternoon and its winds clogged the hotel harbor with lotus reeds. The workers are out there busily clearing a path for incoming boats.

This may be my last journal entry until I let you know I've planted feet on *terra americana*. The next couple of days are "traveling toward home" days. I have various flights and a couple of "buffer" days thrown in between to allow for the vagaries of travel.

I've enjoyed writing about this trip as well as experiencing it. The writing has uplifted my spirit and is a reminder of a path to be pur-sued more consistently. In fact, I am coming to understand more and more that writing is likely a significant part of my current soul work.

And now, Gentle Readers, thank you for taking the time in your busy day to read what I've had the luxury to write in leisure. Hopefully these words have brought you a glimpse of other worlds, or maybe a moment of pleasure, or perhaps an insight— of a nature known only to yourself.

2016

Vietnam and Laos

To Cleanse an American Soul

Saigon, Vietnam
March 2016

THIS TRIP HAD an inauspicious beginning even before I left the U.S.

My airport ride called to say that flashing squad cars had cordoned off my street—unheard of in my 30 years in that location—and asked would I bring my bags down the street. Okay, okay, I said to myself, let's get those unavoidable little travel inconveniences over and done with right away. (Ha!)

I had recently discovered that, once again, I possessed enough points on my airline mileage plan to journey in comfort almost anywhere in the world, but it was one country in particular that called to me—Vietnam.

As an American it was another "pilgrimage" for me. I wanted to see the current status of a country where so much American and Vietnamese blood had been shed over a vague and controversial cause. I also hoped to replace those graphic images of conflict and suffering I had seen on the evening news for so many years—and cleanse my American soul a bit—by seeing a unified and "at peace" Vietnam.

In the late 60s I had been rather on the periphery of the anti-war movement. As a "minister" I was exempt from the draft, although I wanted to understand more fully why some men resisted it. I once went to hear a young man speak on that topic, but I left feeling it was largely a wasted evening for me. He based his whole rationale of Conscientious Objection on the intricate history of American presence in Vietnam, a narrative so complex I knew I could never replicate it for any reason. After reading more about the draft resistance movement, I came to the conclusion that one's reasons for resisting the draft must be wholly personal. Anyone can challenge a particular version of the history of a war, but no one can argue against another's deeply held principles about not killing someone or not supporting the war effort even indirectly.

A nun friend of mine had deep convictions about opposing the war and decided to act. She was part of a group called the "D.C. Nine" who poured blood on files at Dow Chemical, the company that manufactured napalm. That incendiary was used to defoliate Vietnamese jungles and expose the enemy, but it often fell upon citizens who almost always died as a result, and in excruciating pain. (While water boils at 212° F, napalm generates heat anywhere from 1500° F to 2200° F.)

My friend spent time in jail because of her action, and at first I wondered how I'd have responded had she asked me to join that protest. Deep down though, I know I wouldn't have participated in it. My personality doesn't lend itself to be an "activist." In the AIDS crisis of the 80s and 90s, I was not one who protested in front of pharmaceutical companies or who had lain down in streets during a group die-in. I was in the back room giving comfort, hopefully, through massage to those battered bodies that were the casualties of the epidemic. That was my strength, my contribution. Since "activism" was not my style, the only support I mustered for the anti-war effort in the 60s and 70s was being the occasional sympathetic ear to those more actively involved.

This trip to Vietnam, I think, is in part saying, "I'm sorry I didn't do more."

Saigon, Saigon! The city lies sweating at a latitude of 16 degrees N—think Central America—although tonight, my second night here, wind, wind, wind from somewhere has swept the sultriness away and with it the heaviness I feel in such weather.

I write this on the verandah of the Sunland Hotel, a medium level hotel not exactly in the heart of things. As with most such hotels, which I chose to fit my budget, I was at first disappointed but am becoming quite fond of it. The staff is very helpful, the small pool on the 12th floor is crystal clear, and the morning breakfast buffet—mainly Western style—suits me. My stomach likes familiar food in the morning, but I must say I love the tasty fried rice that takes the place of hash browns.

The currency exchange is about 22,000 dong to 1 USD, but it really takes only about a day to adjust mentally to the math required—though at first it can be daunting.

On arrival at the airport I had asked a friendly looking guy near the ATM which button I should choose for 300 USD.

"You press six million, please."

I smiled as I waited outside for a taxi, feeling like a millionaire.

That smile disappeared about an hour later when I realized I had left my debit card in the ATM. Am I getting too distracted to travel alone anymore?

The empathetic girls at Reception said they were so sorry but assured me all was lost. Ken, the doorman/bellhop, advised me to quickly call my bank and cancel the card. A German couple was succinct. "*Kaputt*. Finished, finished."

Was no one offering hope? One's debit card is *the* source of money when traveling in Asia. I can pay for a $3 cup of coffee on my credit card in the U.S. or in most of Europe, but not here. Outside the hotel, cash is what counts and one's debit card gives you that good stuff right here right now. That little coffee stand in Saigon doesn't have a credit card reader, no surprise.

My mind ran through options: take the long chance and return through noisy and chaotic streets to the airport, or resign myself to having money wired to me and carrying around a large cache of cash. I leaned toward going the airport route.

"Oh, Mr. James, many, many people use those machines. So sorry. You certain you want to go long distance back to airport?" So spoke Lady #1 at Reception. Yes, I said. Lady #2 called a taxi for me.

The ride back to the airport was a major effort at attaining a meditative mind, stopping the "monkey mind" that wanted to brainstorm and process all possible scenarios, actions, and consequences. I was only mildly successful in that endeavor.

At the airport I recognized the guy who earlier had told me to go for six million at the ATM. He directed me to a nearby counter where two shiny pieces of plastic serenely lay there, one of them mine. (Apparently someone else had been careless too.) I yelped for joy and blew kisses in all directions at whatever quizzical faces had turned to look my way.

The lady behind the counter said, "Mr. James O'Hara? Here is your card."

"Shall I show you my passport to verify, uh, prove my name?"

"Oh, yes, maybe good idea."

Yeah, kinda. Bless her trusting soul and the kind souls of those who had protected my card, and me.

I met Miss Saigon last night at the Chilli [*sic*] Pub. She is quite engaging, very pretty, and speaks English real nice.

The Chilli Pub is squeezed in between vegetable vendors on a narrow street that won't normally allow taxis. After I pressed an additional 100,000 dong ($5) into my cabbie's palm, he delivered me to its doorstep. Inside, the place is somewhat classy, with Grey Goose and Chivas and the like lining the mirrored wall behind the bar. This establishment is frequented mainly by Western men who can find it. A whole bevy of leggy hostesses urges them to order more drinks.

Surprised I was there? Me too.

An American acquaintance of mine lives half the year in Saigon and the other half in the U.S. and has done so for eleven years. Right now he is in California and had called me earlier to suggest visiting the bar—he rents a room upstairs—and said he would love it if I could meet his girlfriend, Miss T, who works there.

Miss Saigon, head hostess, informed me that Miss T wasn't working that night. I was disappointed because I had found out earlier via mutual friends that Miss T is more than a girlfriend. The two are now engaged and expect to marry within a few months.

Miss T is 24, American Guy is 70. I had hoped to ask Miss T if she had any cute brothers at home.

Saigon is called the Motorcycle Capital of the world. Its more than ten million inhabitants tool around on over four million motorcycles—anti-pollution masks on their faces—and gun their engines at an intersection in a thoroughly intimidating way.

Saigon is also officially called Ho Chi Minh City but I noticed that the airport code on my plane ticket still is SGN. I have also read that a great many of the residents of this city still call it Saigon in everyday parlance and reserve use of the new name for official documents. My own everyday English will employ the name Saigon.

As night falls the sidewalks become open-air restaurants, served by tiny kitchens in storefronts with corrugated rolling metal doors and which are packed right next to each other. The noodle soups with meatballs look inviting as does every manner of barbecue and steaming vegetables. Most of these meals are cooked on charcoal fires next to the squat tables used by the diners, but I stick with my hotel restaurant for hygiene purposes.

The American War of Aggression

I KNEW THAT before I could truly enjoy Vietnam's comeback from a war-torn land to a prospering nation—replete with green countryside and quaint villages—I would need to first look upon the history of that divided country. A good place to start seemed to be the Reunification Palace, a potent symbol of both the formerly split realm and the now one-Vietnam.

The Reunification Palace

When the North Vietnamese army took Saigon on the morning of April 30, 1975, one of their tanks crashed through the gates to occupy the palace—and the Vietnam War was over.

A boxy structure from the outside, the interior salons of this edifice nevertheless display a decidedly French influence. French Indochina, remember? Built in 1966 for (America's puppet) presidents of South Vietnam, it is in good condition.

The dining room has a curious seating pattern. One table is long and rectangular for guests eating Western style with forks and knives, and next to that sits a circular table for those dining Asian style with chopsticks.

The President had two reception rooms. In one, his chair was elevated above all others and his guest sat opposite him. In the other room, two chairs of equal size sat adjacent to each other for more amicable meetings.

Such symbolism is apparently taken for granted in the diplomatic world. You may remember the constant delays in starting the Paris Peace talks toward the end of the Vietnam War—or the American War of Aggression as it's called here—because of arguments concerning the shape of the negotiations table. I don't recall the winning design.

Closer to home, Secretary of State Madeleine Albright signaled her mood, and her approval or displeasure of another country's practices, by careful choice of the pins or brooches she wore—flowers or balloons on a "good day," carnivorous animals on a "bad day." Once, after discovering that the Russians had "bugged" a conference room near her office at the U.N., she sported a large "bug" pin the next time she met them. "They got the message," she said later. She titled her memoir *Read My Pins*.

The War Remnants Museum

A ten-minute walk from the Reunification Palace is the War Remnants Museum, formerly called The Museum of Chinese and American War Crimes. I was afraid my eyes would tear up so much I wouldn't see the indicting photos on the walls clearly, as happened at the Killing Fields Prison in Cambodia. It was, in fact, overcoming my trepidations about visiting that prison that spurred me forward to visit this museum.

The exhibition hall was packed with people, and though all were reverent and clearly aghast at the atrocities captured in the photographs, it didn't have the same impact on me as had the Cambodian survivor's tale and the tour in that lonely prison in Phnom Penh. I suspect that was because I had seen such photos on the evening news during the war.

Almost more shocking to me than the pictures were the callous and inhumane comments made by American military brass concerning how to brutally treat the Viet Cong. Not that the Viet Cong treated their prisoners gently, but these Americans were indirectly speaking in my name. I felt ashamed. I did not memorize any of those words to quote to you. Such pollution is not for my mind.

While the history of U.S. involvement in Vietnam is quite complicated, one thing nevertheless stands out: while there is truth in stating that our soldiers were there to "fight Communism," deep down it was mostly about trying to contain China's influence in the region. China. It was about China.

April 29, 1975. The last Americans and many of their Vietnamese staff were evacuated by helicopter from the American embassy in Saigon. Perhaps the most iconic photo of that day—desperate people scrambling up a ladder to reach a helicopter—was not taken at the American embassy but at a nearby apartment building that had housed many Vietnamese staff of the U.S. mission. They hoped to make it to the American embassy on that small helicopter to be then airlifted far out to sea aboard larger helicopters to waiting U.S. vessels. Some made it.

Escape from Saigon

ON A BRISK day in Paris in January 1973, the U.S., North Vietnam, and South Vietnam sign the Paris Peace Accord to end the war in Vietnam. The U.S. agrees to remove its troops from the country and the North agrees to release all prisoners of war. An immediate ceasefire is part of the agreement and all parties agree to a reunification of the country "through peaceful means."

But President Thieu of South Vietnam is wary of the vague terms, though he is to remain in office until elections are held. He is right to be concerned, even though the U.S. is to retain several thousand civilians in the country to assist in the strengthening of the South Vietnamese army, and also keep a cadre of Marines in Saigon to guard the U.S. Embassy.

A war-weary U.S. Congress passes a bill in June of the same year forbidding any future involvement of the U.S. in military operations in Southeast Asia. The North seems to see this as paving a road for them straight into Saigon. When Congress, further miffed by hearing of the secret bombings of Cambodia, allocates only $700 million for South Vietnam in September 1974, the South Vietnamese army becomes under-funded, leading to a decline in military readiness. The die is cast. The following month the North begins preparations for invasion of the South.

By late April 1975, Saigon is surrounded by the North Vietnamese army. The U.S. ambassador nevertheless believes the South Vietnamese army will somehow rally and won't announce plans for evacuations of U.S. personnel and their Vietnamese staff—a recommendation repeatedly given him for days—because that was "negative" and "defeatist" thinking, and might also cause panic.

On April 29 the ambassador finally relents and orders personnel to evacuate, but the air force base in Saigon has now been shelled and is inoperable. The evacuation, which had been signaled to key groups of Americans and Vietnamese earlier that morning by the prearranged signal of playing "White Christmas" on the radio, shifts to the American embassy. The compound is soon besieged by thousands of Vietnamese desperate to leave the country as the North's army advances on Saigon.

A number of lower-ranking American officials had for some time, fortunately, been working under the ambassador's radar and sending their Vietnamese staff and families out of Saigon on cargo planes, commercial planes, and merchant ships. By the time the ambassador officially allows evacuation, however, the only means of escape are helicopters ferrying passengers out to sea to waiting carriers.

By the afternoon of the 29th, Marine helicopters—the double-bladed Chinook aircraft—begin the final evacuation. The round-trip flight of about an hour into Saigon and back out to U.S. carriers is carried out amidst the soul-rending moral dilemma: "Which Vietnamese get to go, and which do not?"

The North steadily advances its army and will be in Saigon within hours.

In air bases scattered outside of Saigon, South Vietnamese pilots learn of the evacuation—which apparently doesn't include them—and decide to take matters into their own hands. Jumping into their small Huey helicopters, they race to their villages, land on dirt roads and in rice fields, pick up their families, and head out to sea.

With no knowledge of the larger carriers farther out, they first come upon a smaller ship, the USS *Kirk*, placed closer to land to protect the outgoing helicopters. While the USS *Kirk* has a helipad, it has no space to keep more than one helicopter on its deck. But the many small copters hovering over the ship have little fuel and need to land. Thus, after a helicopter has landed and its passengers disembark, the ship's crew pushes each quarter-million-dollar aircraft into the sea to make room for the next landing.

Back at the embassy, staffers rush to shred classified documents and burn one million U.S. dollars in cash, while the Marines organize the 2800 refugees into groups of 20–30 to wait for incoming helicopters.

The evacuation continues that afternoon, all night, and into the early morning of the 30th. The North Vietnamese tanks enter the city at dawn, as the last remaining group of eleven Americans—Marines—sits quietly on the embassy roof, watching the tanks roll in and praying they don't open fire.

Knowing that only one more helicopter would be coming in, the Marines had silently filed up to the rooftop in those early hours and barricaded access to the roof, while some 400 Vietnamese still remained in the courtyard.

The last helicopter finally arrives and lifts the remaining Marines off to safety just as desperate Vietnamese—most of them former employees of the U.S.—enter the building, climb the stairs, and futilely pound on the locked door.

Ken, and the Little Emperor

WHEN I HAD arrived at the Sunland Hotel my first day in Saigon, Ken took my bags and led me toward the elevator after check-in. The elevator door opened onto the lobby and a young Western woman charged forth with long bamboo-somethings poking out of her backpack. These would have hit Ken in the face had he not instinctively stepped aside. The woman appeared not to notice anything and made straight for the reception desk.

The look on Ken's face was distressing. I thought it said, "She treated me like I wasn't even there." At least that is what I would have concluded. I leaned toward him and said, "I'm sorry." He said it was okay but his face didn't match his words. He brightened as we chatted in my room, and now he always has a ready smile for me, and an occasional hint.

"Please remember to hold your shoulder bag in front of you. Someone might try to steal it from behind." When I had returned from the airport with my precious debit card, his smile had been the most radiant of all.

I have encountered this before, taking hotel staff for granted, or worse, treating them as non-entities. I cannot claim total innocence in this matter. And I must be careful about judging the young woman. She may have been anxious and distracted about catching an international flight, or perhaps desperate to retrieve a debit card carelessly left at an ATM.

While perusing my hotel room's brochure of places to visit in Saigon, I noted the high marks it gave to The Jade Emperor's Pagoda. The description said that it "must not be given away." Translation, I think: not to be missed.

In Taoism the supreme god is the Jade Emperor or the King of Heaven. This temple in Saigon is a vibrant and incense-filled place of worship, and houses divinities carved in dark wood, some of the 12–15 feet high. On many of the altars you can find bottles with oil for the oil lamps. For a small donation, you can add more fuel to the lamps.

Churches, Buddhist and Hindu and Taoist temples, synagogues, almost every place of worship have candles lit by the custodians and ones available for the faithful to light. What attracts us to want to light candles? The most common interpretation is that the candle is used for *prayer intentions* for another person. We wish them health or safety or, in the case of the dead, swift passage through the anterooms of heaven/paradise.

In the Book of Exodus reference is made to keeping a lamp perpetually lit to have continuous "incense before the Lord" for all generations. Light was also a symbol of the presence of the Lord himself, and "Let there be light" was the first command in the imposing of order on chaos.

The list goes on as to the various symbolisms of light and lighting candles, but two thoughts came to me as I pondered if I should add oil to the lamps.

First, when we burn a candle we are "using something up." It's that old sense of sacrifice, that it is good to give up something in return for favors asked. The story of Cain and Abel long ago instructed us how best to sacrifice goods to gain divine blessing, and we learned not to skimp on what we offered.

My second thought was that although candles actually illuminate the dark recesses of a church or temple—their initial purpose—many of us may have lost appreciation for that basic function. Our electric lamps, in various forms, brighten up any room instantly and also provide art and decoration for us, especially around holidays.

I love the conveniences of electricity, believe me, but it might be good for us to camp more often by the seashore or trek in the wilderness, or visit villages in the hinterlands of foreign countries where candles or kerosene lamps are all one has after dark. What an increased appreciation we might then have of candles—and of light.

I finally decided not to add oil to the lamps after giving a donation. I didn't want any local person to feel I was imposing myself into their religious traditions without really knowing what I was doing. Such an action might seem offensive to a few. Unless invited to participate—as I had been at the Shwedagon stupa—I'd rather take the cautious route in the matter.

This Taoist temple is relatively small though a shaded garden in front contains several multi-trunked banyan trees and benches for relaxing. I sat down on one bench, at the other end of which was a young woman and beyond her, her small son, perhaps a four-year-old.

I indicated that I wanted to take a picture of him and the mother nodded agreement.

But the young scamp wasn't having it and played peek-a-boo behind his mother's shoulder. Finally I pretended to focus on taking a picture of the tree above him, and when he emerged from hiding I got my photo.

He laughed and I was pleased he wasn't irritated by the ruse. A few minutes later he approached me, his cupped hands full of peanuts in the shell for my enjoyment. I thanked him, and later happily practiced counting "1, 2, 3" with him in English at his mother's instigation.

That kid outshines any emperor, jade or otherwise.

A Town Preserved In Time

I HAD WANTED to spend a couple days in the important city of Saigon, and a couple was enough. That high-octane metropolis is exhausting. I escaped from Saigon on an Airbus A321, not a helicopter.

About an hour and a half away on Vietnam Airlines lies the central coastline town of Hoi An, and I am now relaxing in my second-floor suite at Wind Bell Villas. This is a lovely family-run resort. Three generations zip around handling various tasks, and one of the small kids sounds like a jungle bird constantly cawing. His antics are more charming than you might think.

The town is a village preserved in the past, with most houses and buildings as they were several hundred years ago before this place lost its prominence as the premiere port in the area. Although Hoi An grew to high importance as a trading center in the early 17th century and on into the 18th, by the end of that latter century it went into quick decline. A new clan of warring lords had overthrown the Nguyen rulers, an enterprise they were aided in by the French. The new emperor repaid the French for their help by giving them exclusive trade rights to the nearby port of DaNang, a half hour north of here and currently home to the area airport.

The old warehouses with tiled rooftops—such as you saw in *Crouching Tiger, Hidden Dragon*—have been turned into cute tea shops, boutique hotels, and restaurants. Hoi An is a World Heritage Site and is considered the most charming town in Vietnam.

My room is about 25 feet long and 15 feet wide, plus a balcony which runs that whole length. I don't need all this space but that's what was available. $55 per night.

On my first afternoon here I met an early 30s American guy at the pool with a Hindi saying tattooed on his arm. I was able to read most of it (basically, "live and let live") and he was duly impressed. Jordan and I found we had much to talk about, especially his travels in India and, small world story, his mother lives around the corner from me in Berkeley.

Later he asked me to join him for dinner if I didn't have plans. At the pool he had said that he worked in a restaurant in Chicago so I figured he knew his food and wines. He did. We ended up at the town's #1 restaurant, at least according to both the guidebook and the French couple at the table next to us who live here six months out of the year. As our sumptuous array of food arrived, Jordan announced that the meal and wine were completely on him. A friend had given him a big chunk of cash just to spend on good eats in Vietnam, and he figured it would taste even better with a companion along.

Wouldn't we all agree?

This medieval town is filled with curious sights in every direction: the covered "food court" with noodle dishes and squirmy fish ready to be offed and fried, alleys leading to colorful temples, and of course T-shirt shops.

I couldn't resist. I bought a T-shirt with the Vietnamese flag on it and the words "Good Morning Vietnam." I never saw that movie but now I must. I thought that was clever marketing, appealing to a phrase known to many people.

It appears to me that capitalism is thriving here. Industrious Vietnamese run clothing shops, restaurants, tour agencies, and more, and tool around town on newish motorbikes. If the American War of Aggression was to save folks from a horrible lifestyle under Communism, I'm not seeing it. Ho Chi Minh had asked the U.S. after WWII to help him overthrow French colonial rule—and quoted both the Atlantic Charter and the U.S. Declaration of Independence in his correspondence. President Truman never responded. Some said it was likely that Ho's letters never reached his desk. Our being Allies with the French would also no doubt have lessened the chances that the U.S. would intervene and help push toward Vietnamese independence from France.

Ho Chi Minh had been enamored with Communism for some time mainly because of its stance against colonialism, especially in the writings of Karl Marx. For Ho, Communism was primarily the road to an independent, free Vietnamese nation, and he embraced it for that reason. The Chinese even accused him of being more a "nationalist" than a Communist. He was.

This evening back at the hotel I ran into Jordan, bought him dinner from the hotel kitchen, and somehow we chatted the time away under the poolside gazebo. The wheels of conversation turned easily, perhaps lubricated by the bottle of wine each of us somehow downed.

Today was my slow day: read, swim, eat, swim, read. I made one foray out to an ATM where, with infinite attention, I withdrew cash—and my debit card.

I have no need to roam the town's main area again. While it is quaint, it is highly commercial. Business makes the world go around, so no problem with that. But I wasn't sure what it could offer my soul.

While splashing in the pool midafternoon, I reminded myself that if I wished to take "soul work" seriously, it must include seeing the "holy" in everything, retail stores included. One early definition of "holy" is "that which must not be transgressed or violated." That is, we should respect *everything* we encounter in our path, both temples and tea stalls alike.

That shop on the corner here is attended by a local person, very often a parent, in order to provide for their family. And in this town they experience a constant stream of tourists, some of whom paw over items and chatter in unfamiliar words. A few might even haggle over the price of an item down to the last penny which they likely can afford but perhaps the shopkeeper cannot.

Even if we purchase nothing from that hopeful retailer, we can render the gift of respect. In a foreign culture where we might not speak the language, respect is often portrayed through our body language. Do we enter the shop with a swagger or a smile? Do we handle the items on display carefully? In some cultures one never offers something to another person with the left hand. Have we noticed that and imitated it when paying for our purchases? Even the volume at which we speak can convey respect or lack thereof. Imitate the manner of the locals.

But how to learn and remember all this? No need to if we truly have respect deep in our hearts. The proper or at least acceptable actions will follow. And should we make a misstep, let's forgive ourselves and learn.

It crossed my mind to get out of the pool, walk into town, and test myself on these attitudes and practices. But I didn't. I'm lazy today.

When I emerged from those cooling waters, I sat under the gazebo to write in my journal.

Oh, that little boy who imitates birds just appeared from behind a large wicker chair to stare at me. I waved at him, but he scurried away with more cawing. He makes me laugh.

Why am I so entranced by these young kids? Besides the simple fact that they are entertaining, they are new life, innocent, and always a sign of the future. Perhaps paying attention to them even slightly is a nurturing act. I suspect most of us, with or without progeny, have this hard-wired desire to nurture the next generation—or the generation after that, since I am now in the "grandfather" generation.

Years ago I indeed took on the project of generating and nurturing the "next generation" of members, in India, of the Brotherhood I had belonged to. My visits back to Asia in 2002 and 2006 happily allowed me to see the development of those young men and the educational works for the poor they engage in. How blessed I am to have seen those results.

I do not have any biological children, though I was once offered that possibility.

"Jim, I have a proposition for you."

I was sitting in the teachers' office at the massage school, going over my notes for the next class. About ten minutes before class time, another instructor, Suzanne, had entered the office and sat across from me.

I made some lame joke about her "propositioning" me on campus, but Suzanne just smiled. A skilled and well-liked instructor, Suzanne could handle almost any classroom situation without missing a beat in her presentation, or stop a potential mugger in the parking lot at night with assertive commands like "I have nothing for you! I have nothing for you!" She simultaneously exuded poise and power.

"My partner Maria and I hope to have a baby, so we're looking for a sperm donor. I thought of you."

I was caught off guard. I had never even fantasized that scenario before.

"Oh, oh heavens. Uh, I'd have to think about that. But I am honored that you asked."

"Of course you needn't decide right now."

Yeah. Not when I have to teach a class in Deep Tissue (which we instructors liked to call "Deep Issue") in a few minutes.

"I admire you and respect you, Jim, and would love it if you'd consider this. There would have to be tests concerning your sperm count and general health, but I do hope you'll think about it. And you could be involved as little or as much in co-parenting as you like. I'm sure we could work out the details."

We talked for just another minute or so and I assured Suzanne I would seriously think about what she'd asked. I entered my classroom in a rather distracted state, quite unusual for me.

Over the next few days I pondered what it would mean to father a child at my age and my status as a single gay man. I was in my early fifties, not that old physically. My own father had his last child when he was 52. But would I want to be partially involved in raising a teenager in my sixties? Would I want to be involved at all?

Eventually what became clear to me was this: I simply could not knowingly have a child in the world and *not* participate in its upbringing. And no, I really didn't want even minimal responsibilities for child-rearing at that point in my life. I didn't make a list of pros and cons on the subject, I just *knew*. What "sits right" in the gut over time is a powerful indication of how to proceed in many situations.

When I told Suzanne of my decision, she thanked me for considering her request and said she understood. I assured her again that I was honored to have been asked, and I wished her good fortune in her important endeavor.

I also mentally thanked Suzanne any number of times in the ensuing weeks for giving me the chance to ponder the real possibility of parenthood, something I had given no thought to previously. What a challenging discussion—about having children or not, and if so, how many—it must be for couples to have when choice in this matter is possible.

I don't regret my decision to not attempt parenthood. I'll just sit back, as grandparent-generation folks should, and enjoy the children that others bring into the world and care for oh those many years.

And I am profoundly grateful to have gotten to this particular generational age in my life. Years ago my eyes were opened to what a blessing it is to age, even with its aches and pains.

A Poignant Lesson

It was the summer I was turning fifty, and I must have been listening to way too many people moan about aging.

"Oh, Mark," I said to a younger friend of mine. "In a few months I'll be fifty! I thought forty was over the hill, but now, fifty, oh god."

I should have known better than to carry on like that—Mark, looking pale, was HIV positive.

He looked at me with tired eyes and said simply, "Lucky you. You get to be fifty."

I was stopped in my tracks, didn't know what to say. I would like to report that I grabbed his hand and thanked him for the great gift of awareness he had just given me. But I didn't. I just stood there, speechless, then gently nodded my head. I think, I hope, he understood that I was grateful to him.

Mark never made it to fifty and was too sick to come to my birthday party that year. I was there at the hospital in his last days, and was the person to officially approve "pulling the plug" as per the wishes he had explained previously.

To this day I see his face and hear his voice when I am tempted to feel sorry for myself. What he taught me that day may be the only major life lesson I believe I "got" the very first time around.

Rest in peace, Mark, my teacher.

Final Evening Under the Gazebo

Last night Jordan and I were joined for a poolside dinner by two mid-fifties women from New Zealand, Di and Jennie. They had announced to their less-adventurous husbands that they were going on a trip and had organized a lovely three-week holiday tour of Vietnam.

On a whim I asked and, sure enough, their favorite movie is *Shirley Valentine*. (Slightly frumpy British housewife, tired of making fish and chips for sluggish husband, ups and goes off to Greece where...) They even throw periodic girlfriend parties back home where they drink, eat, drink, drink, and watch *Shirley Valentine* for the umpteenth time.

Di had earlier that day left her debit card in an ATM and it wasn't there when she went back. Three of you Gentle Readers reported the same thing to me. I have *never* left my debit card at an ATM in the U.S. What *is* it with us when we travel?

Jennie had brought a bottle of brandy to the table and a good time was had by all.

Food. I love what they call White Rose here: steamed rice noodles stuffed with pork and shrimp, and a side of fish sauce to sharpen its taste—yum. Only one downside so far, Vietnamese coffee. A thick syrupy concoction to which they add sweetened condensed milk. Sorry, but yuck.

Tomorrow Jordan is off on a five-day motorcycle tour of the central highlands with a group called EasyRiders. The itinerary sounds quite adventurous: ride, fish, stay in people's homes, learn to cook with them, get a real sense of local life. A bit too rustic for me. But then, he is thirty-one and I will (happily) turn seventy-five this year.

The Hanoi Elite Hotel and
"The Hanoi Hilton"

AN ANCIENT CAPITAL and now a sprawling city, Hanoi has many homes and buildings of French-style architecture, as well as an Old Quarter. The latter is a rabbit warren of winding streets which I have not yet quite figured out, though that is the location of my hotel.

The Hanoi Elite Hotel is charming and cozy and is reached by walking down an alley, which is so narrow that no cars are allowed. When you arrive from the airport by taxi at a nearby actual street, the cabbie whips out his mobile phone, calls the hotel, and presently a young man appears at your vehicle to carry your bags.

The hotel's concierge was quite helpful in getting me settled in my room—where the large bed was strewn with flower petals—and mentioned several sights I must see. At the top of the list was Ho Chi Minh's mausoleum.

The Mausoleum
This place is definitely a pilgrim's destination judging by the hundreds if not thousands of people, half of them schoolchildren, in line waiting to enter the sacred precincts. One cannot walk on

the sizable square in front of the entrance and should you not know that or forget your place, policemen will quickly shoo you off. You can be either part of the interminable line, or take pictures from across the square. Those in the queue must observe a list of rules: no shorts or miniskirts, no talking in line, no smoking, and no hands in the pockets or arms crossed. I chose to take photos from a distance since the wait to enter the structure itself was about two hours.

Inspired by Lenin's mausoleum, the chunky tomb and its outer buildings are impressive. They dwarf everything in their surroundings and indeed inspire awe. Inside, the guidebook says, Ho Chi Minh's pale body lies in a glass casket even though he had wanted a simple cremation. Each year his body is sent for two months to Russia for maintenance.

I can appreciate a people wanting to honor a key figure in its history, but the near "cult" that goes with honoring him, like Mao, frankly gives me the shivers. I wonder if any criticism of these famous men is allowed.

Hoa Lo Prison

Dubbed by American POW's as the "Hanoi Hilton," the prison has a long history. The French forcibly moved a whole village from this spot in 1896 to build the sprawling *Maison Centrale*, the main prison in which they incarcerated and tortured Vietnamese "rebels" who dared to question the right of the French to rule them. The French finally left in 1954. They had been there since 1858, almost a century.

Though most of the prison was torn down in 1990, the gatehouse remains as a museum. The displays—tiny cells, a guillotine, other unmentionables—are primarily about the French atrocities. At the end of the tour, two rooms showcase the experience of American POW's, mainly pilots shot down over North Vietnam.

Photos show these American prisoners playing basketball and chess, celebrating Christmas, eating tasty food—having just a jolly good time it would seem. The placards repeatedly state how great the accommodations were, how humane the Vietnamese were to their prisoners. No mention is made of stressful interrogation techniques, or tortures like rope bindings, irons, beatings, and prolonged solitary confinement. John McCain's jumpsuit and parachute are on display in a glass box.

Walking back to my hotel, I stopped to admire a French colonial structure with a large garden in front. I heard an American voice behind me, so I turned and asked the young man if he knew what the building was. No, but...chat, chat...he is from my home town of Milwaukee and used to attend elementary school at St Matthias Church where I had been baptized many decades earlier. How does this stuff work?

My favorite explanation of "synchronicity" is that such events reflect the ongoing deep-level connectedness of all humanity, of which we are able to get a glimpse when these occurrences are thrust upon us.

A cherished image of mine for grasping this connectedness is the Great Fabric of Life. Each of us is a thread in that ensemble and no fabric would exist without the threads. If we would pull long enough on a loose thread of a knit shirt, eventually we will have a heap of thread but no shirt.

The ancient Chinese seem to have understood this. Many Westerners have heard of the energy lines or "meridians" that are a key part of Traditional Chinese Medicine, but the word "meridian" can be misleading. That term was originally used in the West as another name for the imaginary longitudinal lines on our globe. Thus we might be inclined to think of the acupuncture meridians as lines "on" the body.

True, each meridian has its own defined pathway, but it is not "separate" from the body as a whole. The original word in Chinese, I'm told, is more accurately translated as "thread." And there we have it: just as a fabric cannot exist separately from its threads, the living, functioning body would cease to be such without these energy flows.

The Great Fabric, like a knit shirt, has seemingly separate threads which are really all one thread looping around and around. No surprise then that we find ourselves meeting a bit of our own history, even in faraway places.

The Great Fabric is an analogy, and analogies have some characteristics in common, others not. No matter. Even the best analogy cannot do justice to the reality. Remember Rumi? "Language is a tailor's shop where nothing fits."

Imagine

Having visited the prison earlier today, major issues like freedom and war have been on my mind. So it wasn't a surprise when, at Tom's StreetSide Bar tonight, those topics came up when chatting with an Australian couple at the next table. We spoke of war and politics, from tragedy to Trump—not a big leap.

Popular Western songs had played over the loudspeakers all evening and at one point a set of Beatles recordings came on. I loved hearing the mellow tones of "Hey Jude," but it was when they played John Lennon's "Imagine" that I melted. Do you remember the words? He sings about a world with no separate countries, nothing to kill or die for, no religions separating us.

Amen.

"Dragons Descended to These Waters"

Ha Long Bay, Gulf of Tonkin

I STOOD A few yards back from the prow of the ship as it glided ahead, the forward mast and rigging only partially blocking my view.

On either side of us rock formations appeared in the afternoon mist, sheer limestone cliffs rising out of the Gulf of Tonkin thirty to several hundred feet high. We slowly passed them to reach seemingly open waters only to find hundreds more rock islands all around us. This landscape continued to envelop us, its breadth and depth hidden by the fogginess.

I had first seen images of this area in the film *Indochine*. Toward the movie's end, the young lovers escape their pursuers by hiding in this strange and mystical land. I decided then that I wanted to see it for myself.

Our boat carries 30–35 of us passengers and we stay overnight in cabins with dark wooden interiors and all the amenities of a good hotel room—except for spaciousness. But I'm not complaining. My room even has a small private deck where I can sit to enjoy the sunset.

Apparently I am an anomaly to both foreigners and locals, for different reasons. To other foreigners, it seems strange that I don't carry a mobile phone or tablet. I am not wired and choose not to be. Back at home one of you had suggested that I get a

Skype account so I can speak with you economically while on this trip. If you are receiving this email, you already know of my affection for you, so you won't take it amiss when I say I'm not interested in talking with you these days. I mainly want to be Here.

Local guides seem astounded that I am traveling alone. "Aren't you lonely? Are you bored?" Remember, many Asian folk like to be in groups, especially family groups, so they wonder about me. What type of social being could I possibly be?

I'd wager that I have connected with more people on this ship than anyone else. And not just in passing, as in the few words of greeting in Spanish I mustered for that group. I've had great conversations with almost everyone, especially the Australian couple seated at the dining table next to me, Angela and Nigel. Aussies are everywhere. He pronounces his name almost like "nodule."

I was indeed the only "single" on board the first day. The second day, a young Canadian woman, Julianne, joined the ship. They put us "singles" at tables adjacent to each other, but not across from each other. We could turn to the side to talk, or not. Rather adroit, I'd say.

Laos

Luang Prabang

SOME COUNTRIES STILL have those Arrival forms that ask you for information you don't have, such as the name of your contact in the country or the phone number of your hotel. Vietnam does not use them, Laos does.

When I arrived at Immigration in Luang Prabang, the old capital of Laos, their Arrival form asked a question I have never seen on any such card before—Race. Really? The point? Though I was tempted to put down Human, I wrote White. The space allotted was too teeny for Caucasian, and I'm not even sure what the "proper" terms are these days.

The Old Town of Luang Prabang is situated on a peninsular-shaped piece of land, formed by the mighty Mekong on one side, and a sizable tributary, the Namkhan, on the other side. Three main parallel streets run the length of the narrow town with hotels facing the two rivers, and the middle road containing hotels, restaurants, temples and monasteries, the old palace, and more temples and monasteries.

My hotel, the Apsara, faces the Namkhan and my second-floor room offers a great view of the greenish river. On the other side of town, the Mekong runs swift and brown.

If there is a charming town to rival Vietnam's Hoi An, it's this one. I might possibly give Luang Prabang higher marks because the shopping area is much less frenzied and the Lao are truly gentle folk. While shopkeepers of course want to sell their wares and services, the Lao people seem even more concerned that they don't offend you. They speak so quietly and deferentially that I often have difficulty hearing what they say.

There are not really many places to "visit" in this town—the city itself is the lure. But the old royal palace is now a national museum, and is preserved with the same furniture and trappings as the day in 1975 when the royal family members were forced out. I read more in my guidebook about the history of Laos before approaching the museum.

Fourteenth Century to Present Day Laos

"THE KINGDOM OF a Million Elephants Under the White Parasol" refers to the Lan Xang kingdom which flourished for nearly four centuries until its collapse in the eighteenth century. Covering the area of current day Laos and situated centrally in what would later become French Indochina, it had become economically and culturally rich as a result of its being a hub of overland trade.

Due to internal conflict, it broke into three separate kingdoms in the late eighteenth century, was for a period a vassal state of Siam, and became a French Protectorate in the late nineteenth century. Along with many other countries in Asia and Africa, Laos pushed for self-rule in the wake of World War II, and gained independence in 1953 as a constitutional monarchy. Almost immediately, however, civil war broke out and that conflict lasted nearly twenty years.

By 1975, the Communist group Pathet Lao, closely aligned with the Vietnamese Communists, had gained ascendancy in the country and took control of the palace in December of that year. The royal family was put under house arrest nearby, and the king given the meaningless title of Adviser to the President.

The king had been encouraged to go into exile but he refused. In 1977, fearing that the king would escape and lead a resistance movement, the new regime spirited him, the queen, and the crown prince off to a jungle prison camp for "re-education." Versions of what happened next vary, but eyewitnesses and second-hand reports both say the family was made to perform field work and cultivate their own rice. The following year the king died eleven days after the crown prince passed on, most likely from a combination of starvation and malaria. The queen died three years later, and all were buried in unmarked graves outside the camp. No official announcement concerning their deaths has ever appeared.

Today, Laos is considered a socialist country that openly espouses Communism. The government is essentially a one-party system and the ruling elite generally come from a military background.

Begging Monks and Water Serpents

AFTER VISITING THE national museum—which was only mildly interesting—I spent my day strolling the town.

"Vat" or "wat" means Buddhist monastery and the main street is dotted with them every few blocks. These are active monasteries with men in orange robes cleaning the grounds, chanting in the temple, or lining up to receive food from the locals. That latter practice is called the *tak bat* or simply the *bat*.

Signs in multiple locations encourage us visitors to "Respect the *bat*." That is, don't push your cameras in the monks' faces, and give an offering only if you are a practicing Buddhist or have been invited to do so by a local. The *bat* is not a "tourist activity."

There are, however, various tourist activities offered in the area, some called "adventure tours." I won't be doing the three-day trek that includes zip-lining through the treetops to (maybe) see rare monkeys. Having had a close encounter of the worst kind with monkeys in India, a bite on my leg—lo those many years ago now—I still give those simian creatures a wide berth.

Besides passing on the monkey excursion, I will also forgo heading downstream to learn how to wash an elephant though it actually sounds like fun. I could use trunks of water splashed on me in this deadening heat. And you supposedly become trained as a *mahout*, an elephant handler. Really? Certified? Even so, not a highly marketable skill set in California.

I have come to realize that visiting certain museums in a new city can be valuable, especially if you are an art or history aficionado. But it pales in comparison to engaging with local folk when possible, or simply people-watching from a corner café, or sitting silently in a favorite spot.

Thus, on my second full day here I revisited my favorite temple. Yes, I had seen it before but now I wanted to simply rest quietly in that place of meditation.

Meditation has long been a rather elusive goal of mine. My mind believes it's important, my heart desires it, but my soul experiences it only sporadically.

I was first introduced to meditation when I joined the Brotherhood. In 1959, little was known in the West of modalities such as Transcendental Meditation or vipassana meditation or loving-kindness meditation. We were taught a much more intellectual approach to this time-honored path to peace of mind and spiritual insight.

We novices were awakened for prayer and meditation at 5:30 a.m. by a jarring bell right outside my bedroom door. The bell so shocked and unnerved my sleepy system that I set my much gentler alarm clock for 5:20 a.m. in order to be more fully awake when the official clanging began.

Our Novicemaster had explained how to spend the designated half hour in meditation. He would read Scripture—usually the gospel passage for that day's Mass—and then we were to ponder it and have good thoughts. This was meditation?

In all fairness, that practice was often called Mental Prayer, a more apt title for what we were instructed in.

But my eighteen-year-old body had great difficulty staying awake in a deathly quiet room at that hour, and my mind struggled to formulate virtuous thoughts about a Bible reading. Even worse, after breakfast we were expected to write those considerations in a copy book, our Meditation Account. The Novicemaster would later read the account and make comments—"Very good" or "Is this all?"—in the margin using his signature purple ink.

After multiple "Is this all?" comments I decided my Meditation Account lacked luster and I would have to face the issue head on. That was my initial foray into creative writing.

The Novicemaster was pleased with the results. Apparently it never crossed his mind that a good novice would ever embellish sparse, sleepy thoughts with such flowing lines of exemplary and compassionate thinking as leaped off the page in my New Improved Meditation Account.

Good thoughts of course are not to be discounted or ever minimized in terms of our wellbeing. Research in brain science has shown that focusing on positive thoughts actually widens those neural pathways and helps shrink the negative neural pathways. The result is a "happier" person, and happier people are more likely to be compassionate, help others when possible, and lead a more satisfying life.

Another approach to meditation is the opposite of having certain thoughts. The goal is to minimize the sometimes-manic thinking function of our brains. "Monkey mind" is a Buddhist term referring to an unsettled, capricious, or hyperactive mind darting from one thought to the next.

The style of meditation I am most familiar with which addresses this condition is called vipassana meditation, or mindfulness meditation. A simplified description of that process includes sitting quietly, becoming aware of one's breath rising and falling, and being cognizant of thoughts flitting in and out of the mind without focusing on them. The result one is leaning toward is a greater understanding of reality, in particular the impermanence of all things. (Why would I need meditation for that latter goal since I am reminded of the Law of Impermanence every time I look into a mirror and half expect to see the younger man that I still think I am?)

Several friends in California had insisted this style of meditation was life changing, and urged me to try it. We can't really explain it, they said, and continued to press me to experience it for myself. I decided I would.

I flunked my first vipassana retreat. The hours of sitting quietly, an aching back, and the vegetarian food did not appeal to me at all. The five-day retreat was too much for me. I left before the end of the program much to the consternation and clearly expressed disappointment of the staff.

But I'd had more than one moment of an extraordinary sense of calm and wellbeing during that retreat, so I eventually returned for several one-day retreats. Those shorter-term experiences served me well.

But what was happening to me? Besides reading more about the Buddhist philosophy that undergirded this type of meditation, I again sought out what brain science could tell me about my experience.

Literally hundreds of studies have been conducted over the last fifty years on the physiological and psychological benefits of meditation, and the conclusions are similar. Meditation relieves stress, lowers blood pressure, increases a sense of wellbeing, and promotes compassion for others. A key to understanding this is the effect meditation has on the amygdala, the fight/flight center of our brain.

Whenever the amygdala is engaged, chemicals pour into our whole system. These chemicals include adrenalin and stress hormones which agitate us. Meditation apparently helps develop and maintain a "cool" amygdala long after we have finished with our moments of sitting quietly. The real benefit from meditation then is these longer-lasting effects. We will have re-programmed ourselves to cruise along in calm overdrive all day long without having to think about it.

It's the self-discipline of creating a "daily practice" that seems to be my downfall.

I had lunch today at the Three Nagas, an upscale restaurant in the middle of town. I asked the hostess if *naga* meant "snake" as it does in Sanskrit. She said yes and that snakes, actually water serpents, are a symbol of Laos. Remember, in this part of the world serpents and dragons are auspicious creatures, and *nagas* live in the rivers that are a source of water for humans and for crops.

You may recall that in the Harry Potter books, the giant slithering snake was called Nagini. Rowling has this talent for naming her characters, places, and things in clever and evocative ways.

The hostess was a young French woman with that accent so many of us love. (I am one-fourth French but I speak only Amur'can.) She wore a slinky, short dress that would have prevented her from visiting the Buddhist temple around the corner, but I suspect temple-hopping is not mademoiselle's priority.

And the day came to an end with another visit to my favorite temple, a structure painted brightly in stunning gold and red hues, but an oasis of calm.

I am slowing down in life. I'm quite healthy, but don't have the same desire to see more and more places as I used to, even places of pilgrimage. For someone of my temperament, travel to other lands and cultures has indeed been part of my "soul work," a push to open myself more and more to other ways of thinking and being. Perhaps, with my 75th birthday looming on the horizon, I am shifting to another catalyst for such growth. I know writing is involved. I wonder what else.

Along The Po River

MORNING TROPICAL RAIN. I first knew of it from droplets dancing on the pool surface as I looked out my bedroom window. Moments later that somehow comforting sound of rain on the rooftop drew me onto the verandah. Why does rain usually smell sweet?

I am in Vang Vieng, a small green paradise nestled within Laotian hill country. The five- hour minivan trip here from Luang Prabang wasn't as grueling as it might have been, although we foreigners were packed in there quite tightly. They grow those German lads big and seats that would have been fine for three Laotians had to do for three Westerners. We were a group of twelve foreigners and no one over thirty-five years old except guess who. Fortunately I had booked myself into a Vang Vieng hotel with a pool, and a post-journey swim never felt so good.

Though it's been months since last year's monsoons, the countryside all the way down on the winding road was green, with forests of thin trees cloaking the hills and valleys. In Vang Vieng, the landscape along the Po River is dotted with karsts, those sheer limestone hills similar to the outcroppings in Ha Long Bay, but on land here. You'll get a sense of it when you watch *The Painted Veil*, though that was filmed along the Li River in China.

Vang Vieng is latitude 18 degrees N, like Puerto Rico. So we are definitely in the tropics where heat and humidity rule the day. Tubing and caving are popular here, giving a moment of cooling to sweaty tourists. Unfortunately, several fatal accidents around tubing—because the participants had been drinking all day—and raucous night parties have not endeared tourists to many of the locals. But I hear things are getting more amicable in that realm. Now, charging about town in dune buggies is the popular thing. Clearly this is a place for outdoor activity. Even the hotel's welcome letter acknowledges that the environs, not the town, are the real attraction.

The town in fact is the pits: ramshackle restaurants, dive-like massage parlors with young girls combing their hair out front or picking at their toenails (perhaps I exaggerate), and cheap hotels that only the uber-young would think to approach.

Today's youthful travelers, God love them. They look exactly as they did 30–35 years ago in the Thamel area of Kathmandu, which catered to would-be hippies who were born a few decades too late. The girls here wear the same blousy batik pants, locally handcrafted necklaces of questionable material and meaning, and thong sandals. The guys have the same footwear, walking shorts, and clever T-shirts. Favorite T-shirt seen today: Sakura's Bar, Drink Triple, See Double, Act Single.

Both genders sport king-sized backpacks which go from their butt to higher than their head, and they don't look that happy shouldering those packs of life essentials until they set them down and have a beer.

The other day I ventured out to obtain cash from an ATM, but scurried away from the one with this sign: "For captured cards, call..."

I cycled four miles to the Blue Lagoon today. "Lagoon" is a generous term for that swimming hole, but visitors were having a grand time jumping into it from high tree branches or swinging out over it on a frayed rope and plopping in. Two guys, one from Michigan and the other from Minnesota, urged me to try the high dive, but I just smiled.

Next, I watched several Japanese practice rappelling down a sheer cliff and one of them invited me to join them. Again I just smiled. A local guide pointed out that there was a cave that I might like, up 600 ft. from where we stood, but I would need a "head light" because it's so dark. I thanked him for the information and moved on.

Am I a total slug these days? Back in the day, a trek to Everest or tubing on the Guadalupe River in Texas or parasailing in Acapulco lured me in. No more. The main factor no doubt is age, though one occasionally reads about 90-year-olds dashing up Mt. Kilimanjaro. I still love to hike, swim, and go to the gym, but overall now I'd rather people-watch than do the exotic. And write.

One of the advantages of traveling alone and creating my own schedule is the time I give myself to be still, and write. My younger self surely had no clue that writing would be such an outlet for me and afford me such pleasure. I regularly spend time at a coffee shop or the verandah of my hotel to scribble in an old-fashioned copy book.

Oh, I just noticed that the "Wide Ruled Composition Book" I purchased at Walgreen's in Berkeley is "Made in Vietnam." I had lugged the thing all the way back here to Southeast Asia.

Tomorrow I leave for Vientiane in a private taxi. Yeah, roughing it no longer sounds cool.

The War Is Not Over

THE GUIDEBOOK CALLS Vientiane, the current capital of Laos, a "languid" town that one will miss more than they might think. Quite likely.

I walk the streets of the Old Quarter, stroll through immense, quiet temple grounds, and end up with a glass of wine on my hotel's sidewalk bar. And, repeat.

One place I made a point to visit was the COPE Visitor Centre.

Between 1964 and 1973, the U.S. dropped 260 million submunition "bombies" on Laos, and 78 million of them failed to explode. They lie in wait not far below the ground in almost one-third of the country.

The Ho Chi Minh Trail, North Vietnam's supply route to its troops fighting in the south, veered heavily into Laos, then south through Cambodia. Hence the bombings by the U.S. The bombies are olive-green, almost spherical, about the size of a large orange.

A child might be playing in the forest, a young man harvesting rice, or a mother and daughter cooking the family dinner, when these basic activities disturb the ground beneath them with tragic results. Those not killed are usually maimed for life by the loss of a leg or an arm. Since the end of the war, over 12,000 people have been injured or killed by these UXO's—unexploded ordnances.

COPE, Cooperative Orthotic and Prosthetic Enterprise, is a nonprofit agency that trains people to rehabilitate victims of UXO's, engages locals in the manufacture of artificial limbs, and provides low cost or free prosthetics to those in need. The U.S. government has never contributed to this effort. The mounds of artificial legs and arms—replaced by better ones of more comfortable and effective material—piled high in the Visitor's Centre is a staggering vision of the human cost of war.

On this trip to Southeast Asia, I knew that experiencing Vietnam was important for me as an American, and I wanted to walk the land our soldiers had trod in all good faith and carried out commands from on high. More importantly, I wanted to see that country at peace and freed from the terror that stalked its people for so many years. I had seen that and it eased my American soul—a bit.

But I was not aware of how much Laos was another casualty of that Vietnam/American War. As our pilots bombed several countries in this region, the shards of war ripped indiscriminately through both military and civilian bodies, and the remaining UXO's ensure that the deadly process continues to this day.

The war is not over in Laos. I am left with the feeling that we ordinary citizens on any side of such strife are but pawns in a lethal game that seems, sadly, to have no end.

Who Are We, Really?

IT'S DECOMPRESSION TIME and the last stop on this trip is at a lovely beach, back in Vietnam.

Nha Trang is the Acapulco of Vietnam. Its three and a half-mile crescent-shaped beach lined with hotels and restaurants for every budget is the star attraction. With white sands, blue-green waters, and planeloads of us Beautiful People arriving daily, what more could you want?

My hotel, the Novotel, faces the ocean and has its own sandy area where we aren't disturbed by vendors. The Towel Guy there and I talked about the beach, which slopes rapidly into the water and causes surf to crash close to shore, not the best environment for swimmers. He urged me to try his hometown beach next time which he says is perfect. I smiled and thanked him for the idea.

Staff folks here are quite helpful. When I declined the complimentary beer that goes with the evening buffet, the hostess asked, "Beer you don't like? We shall make an exception. Wine?" Then she uttered in a stage whisper to another staff member, "Bring wine for Mr. James!"

My favorite doorman/bellhop, upon seeing me enter the lobby at any time, brightly and loudly exclaims, "It's Jimmy O'Hara!" Where he got "Jimmy" from I have no idea. "Jimmy O'Hara, do you have plans for tonight?" "Jimmy O'Hara! Have a good day." He cracks me up every time.

But is he genuine or just working for a big tip? I don't know, but sometimes all one can do is to trust. What is the alternative? Always be suspicious when you travel? I'm not interested in that.

On a trip to China in the 80s, I joined a bus excursion to local sights from the town of Quelin. I had been told by the booking agent that the guide would be conducting the tour in English as well as Cantonese since most other tourists were "Hong Kong Chinese," many of whom spoke English. Not so at all. None of the Hong Kong Chinese spoke English and the guide also spoke no English. I was the only Westerner on the bus. I just settled back, watched the countryside, and responded with a smile at the young couple sitting across from me who had greeted me in their language.

When we stopped for lunch, the cost of which I had thought was included in the trip, the young couple beckoned me to sit next to them at the restaurant. They showed me how to hold chopsticks, laughed somewhat discreetly at my attempts, and turned toward me when the bill arrived. All I could do was open my wallet and let the young man take money out of it. I had no idea how much he took, or if the "change" he gave back to me was correct.

But I didn't care. To me it was much more soul-satisfying to trust than not to trust. To have spent half the day fretting about being taken advantage of versus trusting strangers and accepting the *possibility* of "losing" a dollar or so was not a difficult decision.

Is this not how we must look at life? If we are constantly suspicious about everything, we will no doubt find the events that confirm our belief in how terribly the world treats us.

Ultimate trust in life and ourselves is likely demanded of all of us. Regardless of the many versions in religions and philosophies of what happens after death, no one really knows. We simply trust that, just as we have learned to cope with this life, we will cope with the next one—if there is one.

Travel is a vehicle that has so often taught me this lesson of trust.

I leaped out of bed last night in the wee hours, heart pounding, to check my suitcase. All my papers and belongings were intact.

The nightmare which had caused my anxiety I have since titled "Losing My Wallet." The title says it all and that's indeed all I remember of the dream.

I've had this dream several times over the last few decades, not necessarily while traveling, and it usually points to this: losing my current "identity" or some part of it. Our wallet contains those items that identify us, in particular our driver's license which is the closest we have in the U.S. to a national identity card. Losing our wallet and all the evidence of our persona generally refers to an internal shift in the way we perceive ourselves.

I suspect that my "World Traveler" identity is on the chopping block. This trip has been important, and very touching in several ways, but I sense I am finished with long distance travel. My energy and interest just seem to be fading away in that arena. Perhaps I have done the work I'm intended to do through travel and now must focus on something else.

I know, I know, after my last trip five years ago I said I was probably done with travel. But this time the "inner knowing" feels deeper. I'm fine with that identity card turning to ash.

One of you Gentle Readers wrote and said you too had once had a disconcerting dream of losing your wallet. Perhaps your message was what caused me to wake up this morning, my last day in Vietnam, not with a new dream but with another hit on the "identity loss" dream. (That happens to me fairly often, getting up in the morning with a sense I need to go back to some particular unfinished business.)

If I push the meanings of the dream, it might also signify it's time for me to start dropping identification with *all* roles, not just my "traveler" role. But who are we when we no longer are these roles? I am no longer formally a teacher, or a massage therapist, or the administrator of an international undertaking. What is left?

Parents and spouses often ask that same question when parenting or caring for a partner no longer fills their days. True, a hobby or volunteer work can come into the picture and temporarily ease our minds. But those wonderful yet ephemeral activities are not enough to satisfy the deepest questions of identity.

At the same time, the roles we have taken in life are significant ones, defining to a great extent how we "move through life" as we make a contribution to the world around us. What role could be more important than that of parenting? And so many of us are deeply grateful that others in our lives have taken on the role of teacher or mentor.

Nevertheless when we step back from "the role," we are left with that haunting question, "Who/what am I?"

Luckily for us the sages have had the answer for eons. It has been sitting there licking its chops, waiting to see when the question of identity has become urgent enough to listen to it.

"Move from roles to soul," the wise ones urge us.

That's nice and simple, but what does it mean? The first mistake many of us make is to ask for a definition of soul. The Flower Sermon angel whispers in my ear again that the great truths cannot be defined, even if a few words might be said "around" the subject.

We can look to ourselves and accept that soul is our *essence*—that part of us not limited by time and place and intrinsically connected to every other being. The full realization of what that means, and living vibrantly from that stance requires time and perseverance. We can read the great tomes on the subject, meditate, seek a guru, and practice deep compassion. We shall get nowhere, however, unless we keep the question of "Who are we?" in front of ourselves day and night.

Moving from "roles to soul" is essentially about dropping our *identification* with a role, not that we cannot or should not continue to take on various roles during this lifetime. At any age, we have much to give and the roles we assume along the way are important—but not essential. That is, those roles are not our essence.

How curious that the repeating dream of losing my wallet has been urging me to understand that great truth all these years. It's time I paid attention to it.

And now, my traveling shoes are again beginning to feel tight. I must head home to where they can rest in the corner for a while, or longer.

Until another time then, goodbye Gentle Readers—and sweet dreams. If not, a nightmare will do. If it's a nightmare, make the most of it for your soul.

2021

USA

Author's Note

THIS BOOK BEGAN as something quite different from the current manuscript.

After my trips abroad in 2002 and 2006, I received many comments suggesting that the emails I had sent to folks be made into a small book. After my 2016 journey, I decided to take that advice, and started to compile the emails from four trips.

As I read over those travel stories, I saw what the underlying theme was that wanted to emerge: how unplanned events can serve as catalysts for inner growth. Not surprisingly, that led me to observe that same dynamic on home territory as well. In conversation with others, I discovered that many people had similar experiences. Well, then, why not address this common phenomenon through my own stories?

And is that not what our lives are? The many small stories that, woven together, constitute our path on this planet.

While the emails formed the original structure of this book, additional material has been included. In particular, the "home front" memoir pieces have been added, and the historical sections have been expanded upon and in some cases are completely new.

With more time and resources available at home than while traveling, I found myself delving more deeply into the history of each country. And what an enjoyable and informative eye opener that has been.

Although I have made concerted effort to corroborate historical events from several sources, errors may well be present. Even when multiple texts tell the same narrative, I am aware of historical "group think," and I keep in mind that wise saying: "There are three sides to every story—yours, theirs, and 'what happened.'"

In the Vietnam piece, I conflated the North Vietnamese army and the Viet Cong. This is not accurate but was done so for ease of reading.

While *In The Land Of Shiva: A Memoir* was written in mainly chronological order, I chose to render the memoir pieces herein more as pertaining to theme than to calendar.

* * *

It takes at least two mirrors to see the back of your own head. Three is even better, and four is great perspective. My beta readers—David Casuto, Lauri Dietz, Sandy Krakowski, and Mark Massoud—graciously shared their time and talent to point out my blind spots, and did so with both acuity and compassion. Who could ask for more?

Actually, I did, and received additional helpful comments on selected chapters from Coralie Murray and the Friday Night Dream Group.

I am grateful.

Made in the USA
Middletown, DE
26 December 2021

57034069R00182